DISCARD

HOW TO WORK WITH AND LEAD PEOPLE NOT LIKE YOU

HOW TO WORK WITH

AND

LEAD PEOPLE NOT LIKE YOU

PRACTICAL SOLUTIONS FOR TODAY'S DIVERSE WORKPLACE

KELLY McDONALD

WILEY

Published by John Wiley & Sons, Inc., Hoboken, New Jersey.
Published simultaneously in Canada.

For general information about our other products and services, please contact our Customer Care Department within the United States at (800) 762-2974, outside the United States at (317) 572-3993 or fax (317) 572-4002.

Wiley publishes in a variety of print and electronic formats and by print-on-demand. Some material included with standard print versions of this book may not be included in e-books or in print-on-demand. If this book refers to media such as a CD or DVD that is not included in the version you purchased, you may download this material at http://booksupport.wiley.com. For more information about Wiley products, visit www.wiley.com.

Library of Congress Cataloging-in-Publication Data

Names: McDonald, Kelly, 1961- author.
Title: How to work with and lead people not like you : practical solutions
   for today's diverse workplace / by Kelly McDonald.
Description: Hoboken, New Jersey : John Wiley & Sons, Inc., [2017] | Includes
   index. |
Identifiers: LCCN 2017015263 (print) | LCCN 2017030860 (ebook) | ISBN
   9781119369974 (pdf) | ISBN 9781119369967 (epub) | ISBN 9781119369950 (cloth)
Subjects: LCSH: Diversity in the workplace–Management. |
   Management–Cross-cultural studies. | Intercultural communication.
Classification: LCC HF5549.5.M5 (ebook) | LCC HF5549.5.M5 M425 2017 (print) |
   DDC 658.3008–dc23
LC record available at https://lccn.loc.gov/2017015263

Cover Design: Wiley

Printed in the United States of America

V10006187_112318

To Sally Shoquist Dunham
My friend then.
My friend now.
And to your dad, for teaching us
both the beauty of the
written word.

Contents

Acknowledgments

This is my third book and it was, by far, the most challenging to write. There are people in my life who understood this and helped me, in ways big and small. Some believed in this book when it was nothing more than a title. Some of the people who helped me with this book are people I have not even met, though I hope to someday. They contributed their stories, insights and experiences because they believe that when we work *together* with people who are not like us, we become better. I believe this with all my heart, and I am inspired that so many others feel the same.

To say "thank you" feels inadequate. But I shall say it anyway, with the hope that the people mentioned here know that I could not have written this book without them. From specific help with the content, to reading drafts of chapters and providing feedback, to support and love and patience during the process of writing, this book was shaped by dozens of people, and I will never be able to repay all that I was given.

To my editor, Richard Narramore, for understanding "why this book" and "why this book now." For the steady guidance you provide that results in clarity and renewed enthusiasm. For understanding just how hard this one was for me and why. Your words to me on a phone call in early January gave me purpose when I was convinced I was in over my head. Thank you for turning doubt and insecurity into something positive and productive. I am grateful that out of all the editors in the world, you're mine.

To the entire team at John Wiley & Sons, who work to bring us good business books that foster growth, productivity, and better business practices. Thank you for supporting my view of diversity and believing in its power as a business tool.

To Sally, for without your help this book would not exist. I know it's a cliché, but it's true. The hundreds of hours you spent researching, reading, brainstorming, and assisting made this book *possible*. You are truly one of the smartest, coolest, best people on the planet. March on.

To John, for hanging in there and doing this with me—again. Thanks for all your help, support, and thoughtful feedback on the chapters as they unfolded.

To Adam and Diana Fitzgerald, for always coming through for me, no matter how late the hour or how inconvenient. Adam, you've supported me forever, it seems—and now with Diana, I feel I have Batman and Robin on my team.

To Kenja Purkey, for providing articles, insights, and advice at the beginning, the middle, and the end. For always being there. For being game for anything, anytime. For knowing me and still liking me.

To Pam Atherton, for keeping me current on every relevant news article and issue and sending a snarky or hilarious meme or text every 48 hours or so. Please don't ever stop doing that.

To Jennifer Martin, who, despite months of not talking, always understands and is there for me when I finally come to the surface. And to Joe Martin and Jake Martin, my "other family members." I love you.

To Somir Paul, for showing me what true leadership looks like. Thank you for your help and insights and for making time for me, even when you're on vacation and we are 16-hour time zones apart.

To Gillian Power, for awareness, for strength, and the willingness to share.

To Tim Bennett, my friend and hero, for teaching and preaching diversity long before anyone else. And for supporting me and my books, every step of the way. I adore you, Tim!

To Karen Nelson, for being my "mom" growing up and my friend now. For showing me what unconditional love really is. For being one of the all-time best human beings I have ever known.

To the entire team at SpeakersOffice, for believing in me and my message and helping to get that message out to audiences everywhere. Michele, Sassy Cassie, Kim, Jenny: I know I'm a handful, but I'm *your* handful. Thanks for putting up with me. And to Holli, for finding me in the first place.

To Jayne Millard, for sharing your experience and insights with me. I hope we get to meet face-to-face someday.

To Rob Neilson, for sharing your story and the "eight steps." Thank you for making the book better.

To Randi. You're the only sister I'll ever have and the only one I want or need. Thank you for letting me back into your life.

To Becky Carron, for seeing the value of this journey all those years ago—and for seeing the value in me as a person.

To Cliff Bohaker, for your ability to mock me and survive. And to still make the most mundane errand an *adventure*!

To my inner circle, my true family: Cliff Bohaker, Lynne Swihart, Robert Swafford, Todd Young, Ronny Steelman, Carson Garza, Adam Bowden, Andrea Cleverley Howard, Randy McCauley, Gregorio Kishketon, Dennis and Nikki DuPont—thank you for your support and enthusiasm every time I do this. And for the fun and friendship all these years. I cannot believe we have not landed in jail. Yet.

To Kiki, for the hundreds of hours of pet therapy. And to Danit Talmi, for sharing her with me.

To all those who contributed and helped, whether it was with specific insights and anecdotes, pep talks, chapter reading, connections to others who helped or simply being wonderful in my world: Z, Amber, Jessica Hogan, Ben Hogan, Todd Dunham, Mary, Jamie, Tamara, Sara, Mollie, Sylvia, and Katie.

To my clients, who become my friends. You have cheered me on, encouraged me and you're the reason I do what I do. Special shout outs to Ron Arrigo, Bill Rutherford, Terry Young, Joe Jasmon, Kristin Dupont, Jeff Hurt, and Sarah Michel.

And to every reader of this book, thank you for being the kind of person who strives to build bridges and teams. I may never know you, but I know your heart. *Thank you.*

PART I ➤➤

Working with People Not Like You: How to Build Relationships and Foster Connections across Different Cultures and Values

CHAPTER 1 ▶▶
"I Used to Just Be Able to Do My Job—Now I Have to Be Politically Correct"

You've probably heard the line that goes something like, "Work is hard—if it were easy, it wouldn't be called "work!" How true. I don't know anyone who doesn't work hard, who doesn't feel pressure at work, who feels 100 percent secure in their job at all times. Work can be a stressful place these days. Between layoffs, downsizing, "right-sizing," corporate acquisitions and consolidations, wage or salary restrictions, budget tightening and trying to achieve company goals, everyone is doing their best just to get through each week. As an employee or leader, you work hard, do your job and you learn to adapt to change.

But these days, it's not just management or policy or budget changes you have to adapt to. You look around your workplace and your *coworkers* look increasingly different. Different from you. More diverse. You're expected to work with people who aren't like you. Or you're expected to *lead* people who are not like you. (If you're responsible for *leading* a diverse group of people at work, this book will help you with concrete, tested steps and solutions that will provide direction for effectively building trust, resolving conflict and creating a productive team. Part II of this book is specifically for people like you and you can skip straight to Part II to learn how to lead diverse teams.)

Maybe your coworkers are of a different race or ethnicity. Perhaps they hold different religious views. Maybe they're from a generation you don't relate to. They may not speak English well. Perhaps they're from another country or culture that is unfamiliar to you. Or they're the opposite gender and you've never understood the way they think.

Yet you're expected to be a *team player*. In fact, you're expected to *embrace this diverse team*. You're told that your company is progressive and that diversity is good. And, heaven forbid, if you express anything other than *sheer joy* at the prospect of working with diverse groups of people, then you're out of line. Something must be *wrong* with you: you're racist. Or sexist. Or homophobic. Or intolerant. Or inflexible. Or "behind the times." Or you just "don't get it."

At work, it's not okay or politically correct to say, "I'm uncomfortable with this person." In fact, if you do say something along those lines, your job may be at risk. Your company may terminate you for not being on the "diversity bandwagon." So you keep quiet and you keep your thoughts to yourself. But deep down, *you are uncomfortable*.

If you feel like this, it doesn't mean you're racist or sexist or ageist or homophobic or any other negative label. It means you're *struggling*.

You're struggling to understand people or cultures or values that are unfamiliar to you. You're struggling to do your job with teammates and coworkers who may have very different viewpoints or a different approach to work than you have. You're struggling to overcome differences and pull together with different people to achieve high performance at work. You're also likely suffering from what I call "diversity fatigue."

DIVERSITY FATIGUE—WHY PEOPLE ROLL THEIR EYES WHEN THEY HEAR THE WORD "DIVERSITY"

I do a lot of professional speaking on this topic and I have learned to avoid the word "diversity" because of people's reaction to it. I used to do keynotes on a topic called "Diversity in America" and slowly, over a few years, I saw interest in the topic decline pretty substantially. I suspected the reason, but talking with a client one day confirmed it. She said, "It's a great topic, Kelly, and an important one. But I fear our conference attendees won't come to the session if they see that as the title. People are burned out on diversity. They think it's going to be some HR lecture and they've heard it all before. Can you call it something different?"

I changed the title to "The New Demographics" and *BAM!* I started getting booked for that topic like crazy. It was the exact same content, but with the word "diversity" in the title, it just wasn't generating much interest. My client was right: people who work have been coached and conditioned to accept and embrace diversity on the outside, but inside, they're over it. They've heard the lectures;

they've been through the training; and they're simply tired of the subject, even though it's an important one. They have "diversity fatigue." Because they've heard so much about diversity for so long, they tune out. They're either bored with the topic, or they think it doesn't apply to them. They've been hammered at work (and in society) that we are all one big, happy world and that *people are all the same*. But we're not.

Today's workforce is made up of people who come from different backgrounds, different places, different skills, are of different generations, have different religions, values, and cultural norms—even our approach to work can be different from one another. All of this can seem foreign to you because it *is* foreign to you. The only lens you have to view the world through is *your* lens. You only have your frame of reference—you have no idea what it's like to be somebody else or think like someone else. So when you're confronted with someone whose actions, culture, style of dress, approach, nationality, language, religion, sexual or gender identity, color of skin, gender, or age is "foreign" to you, it's no surprise that you may feel *uncomfortable*.

Yet, if you express that, especially at work, people think there's something wrong with you—the "Diversity Police" make it seem like *you're* the one with a problem. You must be "old school" or racist or sexist or "something-ist" if you express any kind of discomfort or lack of understanding when faced with coworkers who are different from you. You may even get in trouble and be reprimanded, disciplined or put on probation if you speak up about any discomfort you feel. So you keep quiet. But the discomfort doesn't go away.

Even those who aren't the least bit uncomfortable with people from different walks of life have diversity fatigue. One of my dearest friends, Robert Swafford, is incredibly outspoken about everything and he never minces words. He embraces all kinds of people, has a wide group of diverse friends, is inclusive and progressive and everything you'd hope a great employee in today's workforce would be. But he exclaimed to me one day as we were discussing this topic, "For crying out loud, can we please *stop talking* about diversity? Let's just go to work, respect each other, and figure it out as we go along! We get it!"

Even if you're one of the ones who "gets it," the word "diversity" still carries a lot of baggage. It's not that people don't respect different cultures, races, ethnicities, and norms, it's just that there has been so much focus on diversity that people are simply tired of the subject, even though it's an important one.

That's one of two reasons I don't like the word "diversity." The second reason is because, in my experience, people tend to think too narrowly about the word. They default to thinking about diversity in terms of racial and ethnic differences.

My definition of diversity is *"any way that you can be different from me."* For example, if you have kids and I don't, we're going to be very different: we will have different priorities and face different pressures. The decisions that a parent makes will likely vary significantly from those that a nonparent makes. When you become a parent, your entire focus shifts, because it has to. Parents think about and evaluate everything differently than people who aren't parents. But that difference has nothing to do with race, ethnicity, or even gender. It simply has to do with parenthood versus nonparenthood.

THE NEW DEMOGRAPHICS

I prefer to talk about diversity using the phrase "people not like you." Every day, you are surrounded by people who are not like you. Sometimes the differences are obvious, such as a different skin color, ethnicity, gender, age, or disability. But there are numerous other ways that people are not like you, and some of those ways may not be apparent until you get to know someone.

Here is a list of some of the ways that people can be "not like you"—some are self-explanatory, others require a bit of description. This is by no means a complete list of ways we can be diverse, but I'll bet there are a few here you haven't considered before:

- Different racial and ethnic groups
  - Black, White, Asian, Native American, Pacific Islander, Hispanic/Latino, Middle Eastern, South Asian (Indian, Pakistani, etc.)
- Different religious groups and views
- Men and women
- Different ages and generations
- LGBTQ (lesbian, gay, bisexual, transgender, and questioning—"questioning" includes those who may be unsure of their sexual

orientation or preference, such as teens who are still developing and exploring, or those for whom sexuality and/or gender identity is more fluid)
- Introverts and extroverts
- Marital status (single, married, divorced, partnered, widowed)
- Parents and nonparents
  - And within "parents," there is no doubt that single parents have different lives and demands on them than two-parent households
- Different levels of income and affluence
- Differing political views
- Different education levels
- Different cultural backgrounds—this would include different heritage, traditions, and customs, but can also include things that shape culture significantly. Examples of these include:
  - Military versus civilian backgrounds/experience
  - Rural versus metropolitan backgrounds
  - North/South or East Coast/West Coast backgrounds
- White-collar versus blue-collar professions
- Differing physical, emotional and mental abilities
- Full-time versus part-time workers and "gig" workers
- Office workers versus telecommuters
  - In some companies and organizations, the flexibility that some employees have in working from home is fostering resentment among those who can't. We'll tackle this issue, and others like it, in this book.

These are just a few of the ways we can be different from one another at work. I'm certain you could add to this list—it's endless. Recently, I was talking with a guy at a business conference about this subject, and he said, "Here's one for your list: gun owners versus non-gun owners!" He was right! Shooting isn't just a sport or activity for many people; it's a culture. Gun owners collect and trade guns, practice shooting, and can't envision not having guns. Those who don't have guns can't envision having them—they see no reason for them. Another guy overheard us talking and chimed in with, "Here's another one: gamers versus nongamers!" It's so true! People who are really into video games don't see it as just a pastime or a hobby; they see it as a complete *culture*. It has its own language, rules, hierarchy, and status. These are two great examples of how people can be not like each other, but in both cases, the difference has nothing to do with race, ethnicity, age, or gender. As you think about your coworkers, what other ways can you identify that they can be "not like you"?

And here's something else to consider: if they are "not like you," then they probably see you the same way—*not like them.*

WORKING WITH PEOPLE NOT LIKE YOU IS THE NEW NORMAL

All you want is to do your job and do it well, without conflict or drama. But there is this underlying level of anxiety and stress that stems from feeling like you have to walk on eggshells for fear of saying or doing the wrong thing. That's because your workplace today is made up of more people who come from diverse back-grounds than ever before. Diverse backgrounds mean that cultures, experiences, views, habits, and approaches will be different. And when you're faced with people, cultures, values, or approaches that are different and unfamiliar, it's stressful. It's out of your comfort zone. It's *uncomfortable.*

It's important to know three things right now:

1. You're not alone. Everyone feels this way! Yep, *everyone.*
2. The discomfort you feel is completely normal.
3. You're not a bad person if you're struggling to function effectively with diverse coworkers.

This last bullet point is especially important. There is so much attention and focus on the value of diversity, at work and in soci-ety, that if you question it or struggle with it, you're made to feel like a bad person.

In my opinion, the very fact that you're reading this book says that *you get it*—you *want* to work more effectively with diverse people and figure out how to overcome differences at work so that you can perform at the highest level. You want to resolve conflict, reduce friction, find common ground, and be the best coworker and team member you can be. You're not a bad person. You're an *honest* person, and you're doing your best to understand people, behaviors, or attitudes that may baffle you.

You are investing the time to learn because you care. You care enough about yourself, your company, your workplace, and your fellow workers to try to make things better. You don't want to just toil away at work. You want to contribute and succeed and be part of a high-performing team. You want to help make the culture at work more enjoyable, productive, positive, and rewarding—for *yourself and everyone else.* If you didn't care, you wouldn't be reading this right now! You'd just go to work each day and try not to rock the boat. But that's not you—you're *trying* to understand people not like you—and how best to work alongside them. You're making the effort and taking the time to learn about how to be a better employee or leader. You're the kind of associate that companies want: thoughtful, invested, and dedicated to positive outcomes. This book will show you how to achieve those positive outcomes, regardless of how different the people you're working with may be from you and how frustrating that can be at times. But before we get into the steps of "how" to do this, let's talk about why diversity is so important in the workplace now. What's driving it? It wasn't always such a hot topic—why is it now? And will things ever go back to the way they used to be?

WE'RE NOT GOING BACK TO THE WAY THINGS USED TO BE

If you long for the days when you could just go to work, do your job, and not have to worry about saying the "wrong thing" to the "wrong person" or being "culturally sensitive," I have some bad news for you: those days are gone. They're not coming back.

If you're part of a minority group, you may have experienced discrimination or felt marginalization or watched it happen around you in your lifetime. In recent years, you've seen some progress in tolerance, acceptance and inclusivity, so you're relieved that "the old days" are gone and aren't coming back. You don't want to lose the forward momentum that society and business now embrace.

Why has diversity become such an important issue for businesses? Why did we not pay attention to it "before" but we do now? What's changed?

Two things are driving the emphasis on diversity: technology and people moving around, all over the world.

Technology and the advancements that have been made in communication have made it easier to work globally. You can talk to someone on the other side of the world, email them, Skype with them, and work with them. When technology broke down the walls that separated us from people in other cities, states or countries, it created more opportunity for people from all walks of life to work together. Back in the day, you went to work in a local office and, chances are, the people you worked with were local too and probably very much like you. *Because you were all from the same area.* Today, technology makes it easy to work with people who may be hundreds or thousands of miles away. You can work on a project with a team of people in multiple locations. The tie that binds you may be work, but the team of coworkers may be completely unlike you.

On top of that, people move around now. All over the world, people are relocating and moving at a pace that we've never seen before. They move for jobs, for love, for family reunification, for quality of life, for their kids, for better climate—you name it. In decades past, people didn't move much because it was harder to stay in touch with loved ones if they moved away. So you had communities and towns and cities where most people were from there. Then they met and married other people who were from the same area, put down roots, and started families in that same area. Few people left, because it was easier to stay. So, generally speaking, there were entire communities where most everyone was "like you"—sharing the same background, experiences, values, language, customs, and habits. For decades and decades, people didn't change much. They didn't come into contact with people who were different from them because they didn't leave their communities. They weren't exposed to other cultures or ways of thinking. People simply lived in smaller worlds.

But all that has changed and it won't "change back." The shift in how people live today, the openness to moving and relocation, the ease with which that can happen now, has created a workplace where people can be from anywhere. That's what is driving the focus on diversity—we are simply coming into more contact with people not like us than ever before. And if it seems to you like this shift happened fast, you're right. It's happened in a relatively short period of time, and that's another reason you may feel uncomfortable—you haven't had much time to absorb it or get used to it. Our society has changed—quite swiftly—and people feel they are expected to embrace these changes and be politically correct, especially at work.

If you feel this way, you're not alone. A poll from Fairleigh Dickinson University showed that 68 percent of Americans feel that "political correctness is a big problem in society." The election of Donald Trump as the forty-fifth president of the United States was a powerful indication that many people are drawn to someone who speaks their mind, without regard to "political correctness." Trump voiced what many Americans felt: that globalism and shifting demographics potentially threaten the life that they know. Whether it's economic uncertainty or a sense that "we're losing our culture," Trump tapped into something very real and powerful: a growing fear of "others" and a fear of being marginalized. The way that he talked and the things that he was willing to say (that others weren't) resonated with many Americans, especially White Americans.

For many people who aren't White, the tone and rhetoric of the election was demoralizing, if not downright disturbing. Many minorities, who have worked hard for equal rights and the recognition of their contributions, feel the mood of the country is becoming less welcoming and less accepting of diverse cultures. They feel the tremendous strides that have been made in the last several decades are in danger of being erased. Instead of identifying with the rhetoric of Trump, they fear him. It may have been politics that brought this to everyone's attention, but *the divisive state of the United States wasn't created by an election or a politician. It was already happening, bubbling just under the surface for years.*

And it's not just happening in America. All around the world, we are seeing a trend toward societies becoming more nationalistic and, in some cases, even isolationist, meaning that countries and societies are tending to focus more on protecting their national culture and becoming less receptive to immigrants, different cultures, and other ways of life. Brexit—the United Kingdom's withdrawal from the European Union—was largely driven by concerns that waves of immigrants were hurting the economy, taking jobs, and changing British culture. Australia is eyeing tough new anti-immigration laws for the same reasons. Many people feel that an increasingly diverse culture leads to a loss of national identity and religious unity, an increase in economic competition for jobs and a decrease in national security. Much of this is driven by fear of terrorist activities. But much is driven by a general mistrust and fear of "others"—people of different and unfamiliar religions, backgrounds, and cultures—in other words, people not like you.

The unfamiliar is uncomfortable. We crave the familiar. It feels "normal" and "safe" to us because we understand it. Unfamiliar people, things, customs, and experiences can be scary, overwhelming and anxiety-producing. They can make you feel uncertain, like you don't know what's coming next. They can make you feel fear, because you don't know what to expect and things are changing, but you don't know what they're changing to or what impact those changes will have on you. They can make you feel marginalized, like you don't matter very much. None of those emotions are very pleasant to feel. They're all stressful.

It's at this point that people behave in one of two fashions: they either seek to understand their emotions and work to channel those feelings into something positive, or they feel resentment.

Feeling resentment is understandable. Perhaps you feel some anxiety at the way the world is going and how fast the culture you've known seems to be slipping away. You're coming into contact with people and values you don't understand, and you're expected to adapt—but you're asking yourself, "Shouldn't they be adapting to *us*? Why do I have to sit through a diversity training session at work? Why do we have to make special accommodations for *them*? Why do I have to work with people who don't even speak the language or speak it very well? Why do I have to monitor my every thought and sentence so I don't offend someone?" You may be thinking, "I just want to do my job, and these people and all these expectations and rules are making it harder."

Or if you are the minority worker in a company or organization where everyone else is "not like you," you may sense the emotions or thoughts mentioned above. Maybe no one says anything directly to you, but you feel their frustration, dislike or resentment and it feels like it's directed at you. The result is that you resent being put in the position of representing "diversity" or being the focus of others' negative emotions.

In either case, whether you're the majority worker who is adapting to working with people not like you, or whether you're the minority worker who is surrounded at work by people not like you, feeling resentful sucks. It's not healthy. And it's not productive to your work.

RESENTMENT IS A CHOICE

Emotions are natural. You can't help feeling whatever it is you feel: fear, anxiety, discomfort, worry. But resentment is a *choice*. You don't have to choose it. Resentment is destructive. It eats away at your insides and makes you bitter and angry. You grit your teeth, go to work, and silently resent that our differences exist in the first place. It's not uncommon to feel resentment. It's understandable. But it *is* a choice.

The fact that you're reading this book means that you've made a *different* choice. *You have chosen to try to understand and work with people not like you.* I won't promise that it's easy. I won't tell you that you won't experience frustration and bewilderment. I won't promise you that it's all rainbows and unicorns. But I will promise that when you learn how to work together with people not like you, *despite our differences*, you will achieve greater job satisfaction, better quality work, better outcomes and solutions, and higher performance for you and your team. You'll feel energized, not resentment.

You've made a choice. You're investing time to learn how to work with and lead people not like you. In the next chapter, we'll dive into how you can break the ice and build trust and respect with someone who is different from you. Our differences in the workplace often prevent teams and individuals from getting their work done. The differences get in the way because they can be sources of conflict and mistrust.

This book will help you focus on building trust and respect with people who are not like you, who may rub you the wrong way. In many cases, you'll find that the ways in which your coworkers are different from you turn out to be invaluable assets for getting work done. Let's get started.

CHAPTER 2 ▶▶
How to Break the Ice, Show Respect, and Build Trust with People Not Like You

It's easier to work with people we relate to and understand. Dealing with people not like us can feel like friction. It's *harder*.

But if you work with people who are just like you, you'll tend to get the same perspectives on issues and that *affects innovation and problem solving*. There was a study done with fraternity and sorority members that revealed this in a fascinating way. Fraternity and sorority membership conveys a powerful group identity and can create a strong sense of similarity with other members of the group. In the study, teams of three fraternity or sorority members were asked to solve a murder mystery. They were given clues and had 20 minutes to solve the mystery and name the suspect. However, five minutes into their group discussion, they were joined by a fourth team member, someone who was either from their own fraternity or sorority, or *a different one*.

When the fourth person who joined was an outsider, the teams solved the murder mystery more quickly and accurately than the teams where everyone was from the same fraternity or sorority. In fact, *adding an outsider more than doubled their chances of getting the correct answer*, from 29 to 60 percent. This is just one example, but there have been hundreds of studies done on the effects of diversity and diverse perspectives at work and they all come to the same conclusion: diverse teams yield better outcomes.

There is another aspect of the fraternity/sorority study that is revealing: the teams that were "diverse" (those that had team members from a different fraternity or sorority house) reported that they felt their interactions with the rest of the team were less effective than the teams where the members were all from the same house. In other words, *working with diverse team members felt harder, but produced a better outcome*.

This makes sense. When a team of people who are alike work together, they understand each other. They collaborate easily, build rapport, and share ideas and opinions freely. There may be little or no conflict, because there's no tension or friction. There are fewer dissenting opinions or issues that are likely to crop up. Everyone's the same, so everyone gets along. It feels easier. It's not like you have to break the ice and find common ground.

Before I started my own company, I worked for an ad agency that had several regional offices throughout the country. I was responsible for managing and running their Dallas office. The ad business is filled with young people and my office was no different—the average age of associates in our office was probably late 20s. Many were single and there was a fair amount of socializing after work. We even had a softball team and we played against other ad agency teams every week in the spring and summer.

We had an open position for a graphic artist and I hired Sam Donato. He was talented, ambitious, smart, and easy to work with. He had a great sense of humor and a reputation for being able to work well with a myriad of personalities.

Sam doesn't walk or stand well. He was in a terrible motorcycle accident years ago and it shattered his legs and hips. He uses a wheelchair to get around. When sharing the news of Sam's hire with my staff, I covered his bio and credentials and told them about his great reputation and the work he'd done for other clients. And I told them about his accident and that he uses a wheelchair. I wanted the staff to know so that they would understand why Sam's office area didn't have a regular desk chair and why the art materials he'd use were being placed within his reach instead of in high cabinets that would have been difficult for him to access.

On Sam's first day in the office, all the employees were introducing themselves, chatting with him, and filling him in on how things worked in our office. I overheard one associate, Tom, start talking to him about our softball team. He told Sam about our wins and losses, who played each position and who was good and who wasn't. Then he said, "Sam, I don't know if you even like softball, but we could use a coach. We're not that great of a team, but we have fun. Would you be open to helping us? Our games are on Thursday nights. We play at 6 p.m., and afterwards we all go out and grab a bite to eat. Want to join the team?"

Overhearing this conversation made me happy and proud. Tom welcomed Sam as a new team member, to both the office *and* the softball team. He acknowledged that Sam couldn't run bases, but didn't make it awkward or weird. Sam was different from the rest of the staff because he uses a wheelchair, but Tom didn't tiptoe around that or make that the focus of the conversation. He simply extended to Sam an invitation to join the softball team, on terms that worked for Sam. Tom broke the ice and started a sincere and respectful conversation with a coworker who was different from him. Breaking the ice is the first step in working with someone not like you.

STEP 1: BREAK THE ICE BY STARTING A CONVERSATION

The only way you'll get to know someone who is different from you is to talk with them. Whether it's a new coworker or someone who's been with your company for years but you've never talked with, the first step is to *just meet them*.

"Meet and greet" is a common phrase used in business, but it's an appropriate one: meeting someone is an introduction, an exchange of names, and, sometimes, areas of responsibility or position. But it's the "greet" part that is so important in getting to know someone who is different from you. A greeting is friendly. It's welcoming. It's inviting.

Imagine greeting guests at your home. You'd open the door with a smile and invite your guests in. Even if you didn't know them well, you'd do your best to make them feel welcome and comfortable. That's what Tom did with Sam—he not only met him and introduced himself, he greeted him warmly by telling him about the softball team and asked if he'd be interested in joining.

When applying this to work, the same principle holds true. Let's say you work in a company and someone of a different race or ethnicity or generation works down the hall from you. Perhaps you know their name, but you've never talked with them. You don't really know what to say, so you say nothing at all.

Why not try the "meet and greet" approach? And if you don't know what to say, here's a good icebreaker: "Hi, I'm Bill from accounting. I know we've both worked here for a while—I've seen you around, but don't know you. Tell me about yourself."

Those four words—"tell me about yourself"—are magic. They're magic because when you ask someone to tell you about themselves, *they will tell you what they want you to know. They will tell you what they think is important.* For example, they might tell you they've been with the company for five years and worked their way up from the bottom. Or they might tell you that their parents are from another country, but they were born here and the first person in their family to go to college. They may tell you about their kids or their dog or that they just bought their first house. Or that they love football and who their favorite team is. They may tell you about their previous jobs or experience. The key thing is, when you ask someone to tell you about themselves, what they choose to share can be quite revealing and interesting. It's certainly the foundation for more conversation. Most people respond very well to someone showing interest in them, and they'll often ask the same questions back to you—a great icebreaker.

What someone shares with you about themselves tells you much more than what you can see from the outside. All you can see on the outside are things like their age, race or ethnicity, or their manner of dress. Those may be important, but *what makes them unique is what's on the inside*. Not all women are the same. Nor are all men. Not all Gen X-ers or Baby Boomers are the same. Not all Blacks or Whites or Asians are the same. Not all gay people are the same. You get the picture. What truly defines a person are their priorities, their experiences, their perspective, and their values. When you're trying to connect with someone not like you, *uncovering their values and their perspective is the goal*. Because once you understand their values, you will better understand *them*. And that will make it easier to work with them, because you'll have a sense of where they're coming from, what matters to them, and why they do things the way they do.

STEP 2: FOCUS ON THE PERSON, NOT THEIR DIFFERENCES

When we meet or interact with someone who is not like us, what we typically see first—and focus on—are the differences. We see their gender. We see the color of their skin or the shape of their eyes. We see their age. We see their style of dress. We note all of these things unconsciously, but they register in our minds as "different" or "other." And often we make the assumption that because they are "not like us," we probably won't have much in common. But it's not true! People are people, and regardless of our differences, there is always something that connects us. It's usually not what can be seen on the surface; it's often something more personal or significant, like family or kids, the size of the city you grew up in, your long (or short) commute to work or that you like to listen to live music on the weekends. When you focus on getting to know the *person* who is not like you, you'll often find that they are not as different from you as you initially thought.

One of my clients is Woodlands Financial Services, based in Houston, Texas. Woodlands Financial Services provides customer financing to independent car dealers. They make their money financing the cars and trucks that the dealers in their network sell. These two businesses—car dealers and the financing company—depend on each other. They can't survive without the other party. The president of Woodlands Financial Services is Somir Paul. Somir is from India. He is "different" from his clients in several ways: he is an immigrant, he has darker skin than most of his car dealer clients, he is Hindu and, although he speaks perfect English, he has an accent. His "customers," independent car dealers in Texas, are mostly White or Hispanic, they're mostly U.S.-born, and I am betting that none are Hindu. Yet Somir has some of the deepest relationships I've ever observed among business people. There is tremendous respect and trust between Somir and his customers and a genuine fondness that has developed over years of doing business together. Why? Because what they have in *common* is more significant than what their *differences* are. Somir and his customers share the same business goals: to create thriving, successful businesses that provide solutions for customers buying automobiles and to create local jobs. These business goals are rooted in their *personal values*: to be an asset to the community, to provide employment for talented people, and to help an often-overlooked and -underserved customer buy a vehicle.

Somir doesn't partner with just any dealer; he carefully vets and chooses the dealers he wants to work with, based upon their business operations and their *values*. He spends time getting to know the dealer to understand what motivates him or her, what their strengths are, what they care about most, and how they run their business. He only wants to work with dealers who are as focused, driven, and ethical as he is. *These are core values, and they have nothing to do with country of origin, religion, or color of skin.* It's not that those things aren't important—it's just that they don't tell the whole story of a person.

I asked Somir how he got started with his business. Like any other business owner, he started from scratch. He identified key car dealerships in the Houston area as potential prospects, and he made appointments to meet with the dealers and discuss their business and how his product offering (financing) could benefit them. Somir told me, "There are no shortcuts. It's about spending time with people, talking about their business challenges and successes, and learning where we can help them. It's important to get to know them on a personal level—that's where the real bonds are formed." Somir asks his clients about their families and their backgrounds. He knows the names of his clients' children. He knows how they like to spend their free time. He can tell you how they celebrate holidays and where they like to go on vacation. The only way he knows these things about his clients is because he *asks*. Somir focuses on the person, not the things that make them different from him or vice versa. He built his business on the "meet and greet" principle and it serves him well to this day. When you express genuine interest in another person, it communicates respect. That respect leads to trust. Trust leads to sharing. You're not going to share personal insights about yourself or your family with someone you don't trust.

How do you build trust? It starts with finding common ground.

STEP 3: FIND COMMON GROUND—IT'S THERE SOMEWHERE

Jessica is a marketing professional with an ad agency background. People who work in ad agencies tend to be outgoing, charismatic, and extroverted. They're drawn to the spark of creativity and the energy that is generated by collaboration. They're "people people." After years of working at ad agencies, she took a job as the marketing director for a small, 10-person company that develops artificial intelligence software. Not only was she the only woman at the company, she was the only one who wasn't an engineer. Engineers are about as different from marketing people as can be. There are no "right" answers in marketing; it is a world of gray—sometimes campaigns work, sometimes they fail. Engineers are the complete opposite: they are highly analytical, cerebral, and data driven. They tend to be introverts. They like to ponder things, mull them over and analyze them, not sit in a conference room with a team of people hashing things out. Theirs is a black and white world, based solely on facts. Things either work or they don't.

For Jessica, even though she knew her new job would be a very different environment from what she was used to, the world she stepped into with these coworkers was still a shock. The guys she worked with weren't just engineers, they were *artificial intelligence* engineers! Total brainiacs! As you can imagine, she and her marketing background didn't exactly "fit in" with this group of guys—she didn't understand them and they didn't understand her! They were a mystery to each other.

Her first couple of weeks there were a little rough around the edges. No one was impolite to her—they just didn't "get" her. And she didn't get them. She'd come bouncing in in the mornings and say hello and they all had their faces deep in their computers, busy solving the mysteries of the universe. There wasn't much chitchat or casual conversation. But after a few weeks, she was having a blast and I asked her what she did to get along with this team of people who were *so different* from her. She said, "I just had to find our common ground. Once you find that, you build from there."

Jessica went on to say that she made a point of talking to her coworkers, using anything she could to break the ice. She said, "I start with work stuff, because that's the area that both parties can actually relate to. Anything can be the basis for a first conversation. Like, 'Hey, is it just me or is our client being more hands-on than is necessary?' Or, 'Wow, I didn't think we'd ever get out of that meeting! Do they always go on that long?' *Anything* to get them talking and engaging with me! It doesn't take much—you just have to start a conversation, and you'll soon find common ground."

Jessica is right. People are people. We all have *something* that unites us. Maybe it's a shared passion, our interests or hobbies, our families, the clothes we wear, where we are from, or current events. It can be something as simple as a favorite food or whether we like the rain or snow! Common ground is there, but you won't find it if you don't look for it. You have to start the conversation *somewhere*. When Jessica was telling me how she breaks the ice at work with her coworkers, she added, "It can be a little awkward at first. It might feel weird to talk to someone you've never talked to before, but you've got to keep going. Expect to feel the awkwardness." I think it's important to know that and expect that—that when you strike up that first conversation, *it's not going to necessarily feel natural*, even if you're an outgoing person like Jessica. That's okay. Start with a simple topic and be sincerely interested in your coworker's answer. Jessica chooses work topics to break the ice—she said there's nothing like asking an artificial intelligence engineer to explain what a "neural network" is to get a conversation going! But almost any topic can do the job. My friend Tamara just dives in with whatever she thinks will be an icebreaker: "Oh, that guy has a Cubs ball cap on? Then I say, 'Hey Jake, you like the Cubs? Me too! How often do you get to see a live game?' Or 'That's a cool backpack that you've got there—where'd you find it?'"

You don't have to agree or like the answers you get. You just have to listen and be respectful. Nine times out of 10, you'll get a cheerful response and it will lead to more conversation. And the more conversation you have, the more you'll build that relationship. Pretty soon, it won't feel awkward or unnatural at all. As you get to know the other person, you'll become more comfortable with them—and they with you.

It's a little bit like dating. When you meet someone and begin dating, you start with small talk. You cover the basics of getting to know someone and perhaps sharing your background, or likes and dislikes. You play it a little safe until you feel like you are on solid ground to share more about yourself. As you get to know the person better, you gradually feel safe talking about more personal details, and you open up a bit more. Over time, the relationship deepens. It doesn't happen quickly, but it happens.

But just like when you're dating, it only works if you express genuine caring and interest in the other person. People can tell if you're sincerely trying to make a connection. But it doesn't have to be complicated or difficult. Here are some examples of ice breakers that may lead to finding some common ground:

> "I wonder if they'll ever fix the heat in this building. Are you as cold as I am?"
>
> "What a beautiful child in that picture. When was that taken?"

"You like Coldplay? Me too! What's your favorite song of theirs?"

"Your necklace is so cool. My dad makes jewelry! Where do you find the pieces you like?

"I heard you like fly fishing. I've always wanted to try that. What's the most unexpected thing you've learned that I would need to know?"

"Your lunch smells so good! Do you like to cook? What's your specialty?"

To break the ice with a coworker who is different from you, here are some general dos and don'ts to keep in mind:

- Make your comment something positive and something personal about them, or if that feels too awkward, choose a work topic, like a project that's under way or a deadline that's fast approaching.
- Questions are good—they draw people out and convey genuine interest.
- Make sure your comments about the job or company aren't gossipy—it can come across as too invasive or that you perhaps have an agenda.
- Ask for advice or ask for something to be explained. Everyone finds it flattering to be recognized for their expertise.
- Find out what they care about, what makes them happy or brings them joy or satisfaction. Or conversely, what makes them unhappy or causes frustration.

Your goal is to find the common thread that exists between you as *people*, not just coworkers. Finding common ground will allow you to get to know your coworker on a more personal level. That's where you'll discover their *values*. And when you understand another person's values, you hold the key to meaningful conversation about real differences in people or groups and how to better work with people not like you.

CHAPTER 3 ▶▶
How Do We Talk about Real Differences in People and Groups That Create Conflict or Hurt Productivity—Without Stereotyping or Offending?

"Don't take this the wrong way, but..."

Have you heard someone say that, at work or in your personal life? It's a phrase that usually prefaces a criticism of some sort, but it's meant to soften the sound of the criticism. It's an effort to be honest, but not devastatingly so. It's an attempt to communicate some kind of discord, but not start an argument. It's walking on eggshells.

When it comes to working with people who are different than we are, we don't just walk on eggshells—we *tiptoe* on eggshells. We tiptoe around our differences and around our frustrations. We stuff our feelings down inside and try to ignore the confusion or resentment we may feel.

We don't talk about any of it—because we're afraid to. With good reason! There are a million ways that speaking up can go wrong for us:

- We are afraid of saying something that may hurt or offend a coworker.
- We think that if we bring up a frustration or objection with someone who is different, we might be exhibiting some unfair judgment or bias.
- We don't want to make our coworker defensive or angry.
- We don't want to "rock the boat"—if we object to the way someone approaches their work, we might be labeled "a troublemaker" or "the difficult one." It seems best to just ride it out and let it go.
- We're afraid we may be misunderstood and be accused of being insensitive, racist, sexist, homophobic, or xenophobic (*xenophobia* is fear or hatred of other cultures and/or foreigners).
- We might get fired!

These fears are valid. In most companies and organizations, there are dire consequences for saying something that can be construed as racist, sexist, or any other "-ist." People get terminated for making comments and statements of that nature. And companies get sued. The stakes are high—for both the employer and the employee. Companies are very sensitive to diversity issues and worker rights (as they should be) and HR departments do their best to educate and train their workforces on cultural acceptance and inclusion.

Most of us aren't any of those negative "-ist" labels. We're just trying to work and earn a living and do our jobs. When we work alongside people who are different from us, the differences can be mystifying to us. We don't always understand why people act the way they do and that frustrates us.

For example, my friend Scott is a retail professional. He used to be a district manager for Lowe's, a national chain of home improvement stores. While Lowe's has a significant number of associates who are women, their workforce is still very male-dominated. It's just the nature of their business: lumber, tools, and hardware tend to attract male workers. For years, Scott worked mostly with men. He changed jobs and now is a district operations director for a large, multi-unit, national *beauty supply* company. You guessed it: most of the associates he works with now are women. He's gone from a very male-dominated company to a very female-dominated company. He is one of just a few men at the executive level in that company.

Scott is a very flexible, adaptable guy, the kind who gets along with everyone and who can fit in anywhere. But he struggled mightily when he started his new job to understand the dynamics of his mostly female team. He said to me one day, "I had a district team meeting this week and we were reviewing sales numbers and each store's performance. One of the managers, whose store sales numbers were below target, started crying. I didn't know what to do!"

I asked him if he meant "crying" as in whining or becoming defensive about performance or if he meant *actual crying*. He said, "Actual crying! Tears! She was really upset and started crying! I was completely taken aback and didn't know how to handle it!"

In Scott's previous job, working mostly with men, no one ever cried at a meeting. Guys are conditioned and socialized all their lives to be strong, tough, and "manly." Showing emotion in a business situation isn't common. But women are socialized in exactly the opposite way: we are taught to express ourselves, share emotions, and be sensitive to situations and other people around us. When something is upsetting, some women get emotional and, at times, those emotions bubble up to the surface. In this case, Scott's associate could not contain her emotions and she got weepy.

This anecdote may sound like a silly example because, of course, not all women get upset to the point of tears at work, but some do. However, I am betting that very few of us have seen a man get teary talking about poor sales numbers in a business meeting. It's just not something most men would do. Men do express emotion, but they're more likely to express humor, pride, anger, or a competitive streak. Women are more likely to express joy, sadness, disappointment, sympathy, and empathy. It's a fundamental difference between how men and women are wired, and it's a difference that is reinforced culturally.

When Scott first encountered the associate who was upset and cried, he was bewildered. He simply didn't understand why she was crying. He was also *uncomfortable*. Nothing in his background or experience prepared him for that. But instead of asking, "Why are you crying?" (which likely would have made her even more upset), he took the approach of, "Talk to me. Tell me what's going on and how I can help."

What Scott did—intuitively—was have a *constructive conversation* with an associate who behaves differently than he does. Instead of focusing on her tears by confronting her or shaming her about crying, he swung the conversation to *dialogue* ("talk to me"), *barriers* ("what's going on?"), and *solutions* ("how can I help?").

Months later, I asked him if crying in a meeting had ever happened again, and he said, "Oh, it happens all the time. In difficult conversations and sales performance discussions, some of my team get a little teary. *They think they've let me down.* Now when it happens, I ask them why they are upset and we talk it through. They tell me what may be holding them back from achieving their sales targets, and I learn what I can do to help them get their stores back on track. It actually turns into a productive conversation."

Amber is a Black attorney. She worked in Kansas City for a sizeable law firm for many years. She once had to do a deposition in Salina,

Kansas. If you've never heard of Salina, Kansas, it's because it's a small town, west of Topeka and north of Wichita. It's quite rural and most of the population is White. In fact, just 3 percent of Salina's residents are Black. The deposition was being held in another attorney's office in Salina, so Amber traveled there to represent her client.

When she walked into the attorney's office, the receptionist took one look at her and said, "You can sit over there and wait for your attorney." She assumed Amber was the *defendant*, not the attorney! Amber replied, "I'm not the defendant. I'm the attorney." The receptionist then said, "I didn't know they let paralegals handle depositions."

Wow. This story and situation offends in two significant ways: (1) the receptionist took one look at Amber and, based upon the color of her skin, assumed she couldn't possibly be an attorney; and (2) when Amber clarified that she was the attorney, not the defendant, the receptionist added insult to injury by assuming she was a paralegal. In other words, it was unimaginable to the receptionist that a Black woman could be an attorney. Surely she must be a legal *assistant* of some kind, right? She couldn't possibly be the actual attorney!

I asked Amber how she handled this. It's an outrageous story and it would be understandable if Amber had gotten angry or responded to the woman in a sarcastic or scolding way. But she didn't. She simply pulled out her business card, handed it to the receptionist and said, "I'm Amber Williamson and I'm an attorney with this firm and I'm here to represent the defendant. I'll wait here until my client arrives."

The receptionist probably didn't mean to make such offensive comments. She *made an assumption, based on Amber's race*. There probably aren't that many Black attorneys in Salina. And the receptionist was embarrassed and mortified when she realized that her comments were out of line. But it's the way that Amber handled the situation that is the valuable part of the story. Amber kept the conversation *focused on business*. ("I'm an attorney and I'm here to represent the defendant.") She didn't make a scene or try to shame or chastise the woman. She made her point, beautifully, by simply *sticking to business*.

People are going to say the "wrong" thing sometimes. Most often, offensive comments are made thoughtlessly, carelessly, or ignorantly, not because someone is mean-spirited. The way to handle such comments at work is to do what Amber did: *keep the focus on business*. Stay focused on the job that must be done or the business issue at hand.

Here is another example of keeping the focus on business when a well-meaning colleague says something offensive. Yves Peeters is the chief HR officer of Glacio, a Belgian ice cream producer. Yves is openly gay. He tells the story of his first day of work at a large logistics company that he describes as "tough, full of testosterone, and steeped in a very old culture." He was called in on his first day to speak privately with a board member, who was very nervous as she told him, "I don't know how to say this, but one of the employees Googled you and found out you are gay. The news is spreading through the organization. What should we do?" Yves replied, "Nothing! Isn't it normal?"

Of course, being gay isn't an "issue" or a work problem to be resolved, but the fact that the board member discussed this with him helped him to see that his colleagues were living and working in a context where being openly gay was entirely new to them and they didn't know how to deal with it. He realized that most of his coworkers had never worked with—or perhaps even known—someone who is gay and that it could present an obstacle in working alongside his coworkers. *It was important for him to know the work culture he was entering*. He knew he had to give people time to adjust to something new or unfamiliar to them (in this case, that he is openly gay). If you are in the minority at work, whether you're the minority race or ethnicity, gender, generation or anything else, let people in the organization get to know *you*. Stay focused on the work: demonstrate your professional abilities, so your coworkers see *you*, not the color of your skin, your sexuality, gender, or age.

Most companies' HR departments do a good job of educating workers about the value of diversity in business and what it means to be inclusive. They provide specific training on what *not* to say. The problem is, they don't always teach employees what they *should* say when they encounter difficulties with a coworker. Here are some tips for keeping the conversation constructive and productive when you're faced with behavior, attitudes, and approaches that are different from yours.

HOW TO HAVE A CONSTRUCTIVE CONVERSATION ABOUT CONFLICT WITH PEOPLE WHO ARE DIFFERENT FROM YOU

This isn't easy. Talking with someone about the differences between you is likely to be awkward and uncomfortable. Add to that, the "someone" is a coworker, not your spouse or friend. You've been tiptoeing on eggshells so you don't say the wrong thing or say it the wrong way. It's time to speak up about differences so that you can function more productively at work, enjoy it more, and build relationships.

For example, a real estate agent at a women's conference told me the story of how she handled a situation with a coworker who had just become a mom for the first time. The new mom was, of course, thrilled with her baby, and it was difficult for the mom to be apart from her baby when her maternity leave ended and she had to come back to work. The way the new mom coped was by FaceTiming her babysitter several times a day to check in on the baby. The problem was that everyone in this particular office worked in cubes—no one had an actual office with a door that shut. And if you've ever been sitting next to someone who is Skyping or FaceTiming, you know that there is *no way* you can tune out the conversation, because you hear both sides of it. The new mom would talk baby talk to her baby and discuss detailed feeding schedules, naps, and diaper incidents with the sitter and the realtor heard every word. There was no way she *couldn't* hear it. At first, she found herself angry, silently fuming, thinking, "How can this mom be so self-absorbed and inconsiderate? She acts like she works here alone! Like she's the only one who matters and the only one who feels anxiety being apart from her child." The realtor told me she liked this coworker, but *was starting to resent her and avoid her*. It was then that she realized she had a choice: either stay mad at her coworker and watch their relationship erode or deal with it head-on.

There are four steps in having a constructive conversation at work with someone who is not like you:

1. Let them be different. You don't have to share their values or like them; you just have to work with them.
   - The fact that you're reading this book means you are already aware that coworkers are different from you and that you're

trying to learn the best way to work together. It's also important that you be honest about what the differences are and your own reaction to those differences. For example, does a coworker behave in a way that bewilders you? Frustrates you? Annoys you? Offends you? Giving some real thought and honest assessment to how the coworker's approach *affects* you is essential. It's the only way to begin a professional, constructive dialogue between you and your colleague.

- In the case of the realtor, she was aware that the new mom needed to have frequent contact with her baby and the sitter throughout the day. It may not have been the way she would have handled the situation, but the realtor was aware that the new mom needed the reassurance that connecting with the sitter and the baby provided.

2. Create a dialogue by asking them to explain their perspective on the broader situation or work context.

- A dialogue is a conversation with the sole purpose of better understanding another person. It is not a debate. It's not about determining who's right or wrong. It's not even about solving a problem—that comes a bit later. It's simply a conversation with the objective of understanding each person's perspective. And *perspective is never wrong*—it's how someone sees things. It's kind of like your opinion. Someone can disagree with your opinion—they may even offer an alternative opinion for your consideration—but they can't say your opinion is *wrong*. It's yours. The same is true of perspective. Your perspective, or that of your coworkers, is *how you view situations through the lens of your own experiences*. It is shaped by your background. So it can't possibly be right or wrong— it is simply how you see things.

- In the realtor's case, she talked with the new mom about her perspective on being away from her baby, how difficult that must be when you have a newborn. She sat down with her coworker and said, "Karen, I know your whole world has changed since you became a mom, and I know it must be terribly hard for you to be away from the baby during the day." The new mom emphatically agreed and shared how coming back to work after maternity leave was the hardest thing she'd ever done. Their conversation created mutual empathy and opened the door to discussing the work issue.

3. Identify the specific issue, obstacle, or barrier.

   • This is where it is imperative that your conversation be rooted in *professional objectives*, and not be a personal attack on the coworker who is different from you. The reason you notice that someone is not like you is because something they do, say, the way they look or dress or the way that they act or behave is foreign to you and perhaps getting in the way of your productivity or level of engagement at work. In the case of the realtor, overhearing her coworker talk baby talk in the office was annoying. But the *specific work issue* was that the Face-Timing was disruptive.

   • The realtor said to the new mom, "I understand how important it is for you to check in on the baby throughout the day. But when you do it by FaceTiming, it's really disruptive to me and everyone sitting around you. There's no way not to hear every word of the conversation and I have a hard time focusing on the work I have."

   • By stating the professional issue (not being able to concentrate and get work done) rather than the coworker's personal approach/habit/conduct (being thoughtless or inconsiderate), the realtor opened a dialogue that fostered respectful conversation.

4. Discuss solutions.

   • This is the goal. You may be struggling with issues that arise at work with someone not like you, but the goal is to find a way forward so you can both get your work done. You don't have to like everything about someone who is different from you, but *you do have to work with them.* After you've talked with someone respectfully about their perspectives on the issue, what the impact is on you, your project or your team, turn the conversation to solutions.

   • In the example of the realtor and the new mom, after the realtor explained what the specific issue was, she stated, "I wanted to talk to you about it and see if we can find a solution that gives you the connection you need with the sitter and gives me the environment I need to get my work done." The new mom did not get defensive—in fact, she was a bit embarrassed that she'd caused a problem and she thanked her coworker for bringing the situation to her attention. She said, "Oh my, I had no idea everyone could hear. I just wasn't thinking. I was just trying to grab a few minutes with the baby throughout the day. From now on, I can do that in the employee break room."

This approach is professional, courteous, and respectful. It acknowledges the other person's perspective or situation without being critical. And it focuses on *finding solutions that are workable for all involved.*

- Here's another example: a small, family-owned bank in Waterloo, Iowa, has a staff with very little turnover. Most of their employees have been with them for decades. When one of their tellers retired, they filled the position with a young man in his mid-20s. The man has a medium-sized tattoo on his forearm. Because this bank is small and independent, they don't have a formal grooming or apparel policy. It's never been an issue before. Waterloo is a pretty conservative town, and the bank's core clientele is primarily older people, many of whom are over 65 years old. Those customers came of age in an era when having a tattoo was something unsavory: it meant you'd been in prison or were in a gang or were a drug dealer. Today, tattoos are simply expressions of individuality and personal stories, but many older people see tattoos differently. That's their *perspective,* and as mentioned above, perspective isn't *wrong*—it's the way someone views something. The bank manager saw nothing wrong with the man's tattoo, but he knew he'd get an earful from some older customers who would find it offensive. He also knew that many customers may not say anything, but they'd secretly be uncomfortable with the young man. The bank manager talked with the young man, explained how some customers might react to a new teller with a tattoo and said, "I want you to get off on the right foot with our customers and have them get to know you. I want them to focus on you and your talents, not your tattoo. What's the best way to make you *and* our customers feel comfortable?" The conversation was respectful and truthful, and the young associate was the one who offered the solution: he suggested he cover his tattoo with long-sleeved shirts for the first six months. He suggested after six months, he and the manager talk again and determine at that time if continuing to cover his tattoos was a good idea. It was a fair and reasonable solution, one that reflected mutual respect and compromise for the best outcome.

These four steps are simple, but that doesn't mean they're easy. The simplest exercise in the world is the pushup. You lie on the ground and push yourself up. It's simple. You don't need any special gear to do a pushup, nor do you need to join a class or a gym. You just lie down, and then push yourself up. It doesn't get any simpler than that. But doing a pushup is not easy.

It's the same with having a conversation about real differences. It's not easy. It's uncomfortable and awkward for everyone involved. But just like building a muscle, it takes time, and over time it *does* get easier. Here are four words that can help.

FOUR MAGIC WORDS THAT MAKE IT EASIER TO START A CONVERSATION ABOUT CONFLICT

"I need your help."

I wish I could claim that I personally discovered how powerful these four words are. I can't. Years ago, I was reading an article on persuasion and the psychology of getting others to do what you want them to do. This article stated that these four words—*I need your help*—are the most effective way to talk with someone and get them on board with a new idea, a solution, resolution of an issue, or almost anything else.

If you ask a coworker, "Can you help me?" you may get a very polite answer along these lines:

"I'd love to, but I'm jamming on this deadline for Steve."
"I can't right now—I have to head into the 3 o'clock meeting."
"I'm probably not the best person for that—you should talk to Cynthia."

But "*I need your help*" works very differently. The article stated that we, as human beings, are tribal by nature: "tribal" meaning that we live in communities, not in isolation. Because we as humans tend to gravitate to other humans, we have learned that we must help each other in order to survive and thrive. In other words, *it's in our nature to help*. So when you tell someone, "*I need your help*" their instinctive response is to say, "What do you need?" It's different from asking, "Can you help me?" That question has an easy answer: "No"! But when you don't *ask* for help, when you simply state that you *need* help and, specifically, that other person's help, their "instinct to help" kicks in.

It's also respectful. And very flattering. When you ask someone for their help, you are acknowledging that they do something well. Whether it's their expertise, their diplomacy, or their ability to think creatively, you're acknowledging that they have a skill you lack and you are turning to them for assistance. Who wouldn't respond positively to a request for help phrased this way?

There's also an element of curiosity at work here: when you say, "I need your help" not only is the other person flattered that you need them, but they are also intrigued. What do you need? What's up? Hmmmmm... Ninety-nine percent of the time if you say to a colleague, "I need your help," their reply will be, "What do you need?"

And *boom*! That's why these four words are magic! Because now your coworker has *opened the door* to a real conversation. You didn't open the door, *they* did! You now have a respectful platform to discuss whatever difference between you and them is affecting you. And you won't make them defensive or mad because *you asked for their help*. Asking for help puts *them* in the driver's seat. They will hear you and work with you more readily than if you just said, "I have to talk to you about a problem I am having."

For example, let's say your coworker is someone who speaks with an accent, and you have difficulty understanding what they say. You could approach them and use the four magic words: "I need your help." When they reply with "What do you need?," you could say, "I like working with you on the XYZ project, but sometimes, I have difficulty catching everything we talk about. When you're really excited and into the work, I have a hard time understanding everything you're saying. And I don't want to miss anything. I don't want to keep asking you to repeat yourself, but I need your help."

At that point, the other person might say that they can slow down and speak more clearly. And the next time you're having difficulty understanding them, you have a starting place to bring it to their attention: "Hey, remember when I told you I sometimes have a hard time understanding everything you're saying? Can you slow down and start over so I can get everything? I'd so appreciate it."

"I need your help" softens any request that follows. Because asking for help from a colleague elevates them. It's an acknowledgment that you know they have answers or solutions. It's constructive because it suggests working together. Those four words truly do work magic because they're respectful.

Here are some phrases that are just the opposite.

What *Not* to Say

It's hard to believe that anyone would say any of the following statements, but it happens. Even if someone is well-meaning, the comments are stereotypical, offensive, insensitive, or downright insulting. I'm breaking them down here by various diverse segments, but I think you'll see how rude and outrageous all of them are.

What Not to Say to Asian and Asian American Coworkers

- "You all look alike."
- "Where are you from? No, where are you *really* from?"
  - Would you ask this of a White or Black coworker? What makes this offensive is that you're calling out their "otherness" based on appearance.
- "Are you a bad driver?"
  - This is a hugely offensive stereotype. Stereotypes are almost always offensive because they lump certain people into a category and ascribe certain behaviors or traits to the entire group.
- "Can you recommend a good Chinese [or Thai, Vietnamese, sushi] restaurant?"
  - A person's ethnicity or race does not make them a restaurant expert.

- "You speak English so well—where did you learn it?"
  - Why would you assume the Asian person didn't learn English at home as a child?

What Not to Say to Black and African American Coworkers

- "You're so articulate."
  - This is offensive because it implies that Blacks are not as well-spoken as other groups and that you are surprised by this person's articulateness.
- "You people…"
  - A phrase that is a stereotypical categorization, whether it be positive or negative, for example, "You people are so family oriented" (positive) or "You people are always late" (negative).
- "I love your name—it's so ethnic."
  - Categorizing as "ethnic" is unnecessary. If you love someone's name, just say so.
- "I actually voted for Obama."
  - Unless you're talking politics, this is offensive because it's introducing an unrelated topic based solely on the other person's skin color.
- "I don't see any color—I just see people" (uh huh, sure…).
  - This statement actually contradicts its premise. If you really "don't see color, just people," then why are you bringing up color?

What Not to Say to LGBTQ Coworkers

- "I suspected you were gay."
  - You wouldn't say "I suspected you were straight" to a straight person.
- "I'm sorry."
  - Being gay, bisexual, or transgendered is not a condition warranting sympathy. It's a facet of the other person—like having blue eyes.
- "What do you like to do in bed?"
  - A statement like this cannot possibly be appropriate in any business situation, for anyone, ever.

- "I have a cousin/brother/sister/aunt/friend who is gay."
  - This comment is irrelevant to most conversations and reduces the other person to their sexuality.

What Not to Say to Women Coworkers

- Terms of endearment, such as "sweetie," "honey," or "cutie."
  - These are patronizing, belittling comments.
- "Is it that time of the month?"
  - This comment implies that the only reason a woman might be irritable is because she's having her period.
- "You're so emotional."
  - A comment like this does not belong in a business setting.
- "You got the job because you're a woman."
  - This is offensive because it implies that the woman is undeserving of a promotion based on her professional skills and accomplishments.
- "You sure you want that promotion? You'll never see your kids."
  - Work/life balance is not just an issue that women struggle with. Most people who work struggle with this.

Holy smokes—this list is offensive! So what *can* you say? Here are a few examples to suggest better ways of talking to your coworkers or asking questions in more respectful ways:

Replace *This:*	With *This:*
What do you people eat for dinner?	What's a popular dish in your culture?
You got pregnant.	You're having a baby!
You must have voted for Obama.	It's so hard to discuss politics these days.
What sport did you play in school?	Do you follow sports?
I always knew you were gay.	Thank you for telling me that.

The reason the statements in the first column can offend is because they embrace stereotypes, painting all people of a particular group with the same brush. Or they speak to assumptions or have a judgmental tone to them. Be cautious about asking personal questions of someone at work who is not like you. *Get to know the person first as an individual* before you start taking liberties with personal questions.

I like the way Somir puts it when he speaks of meeting new people and getting to know them and building trust. He says, "There are two ways to go through a door. You can bust in. Or you can be let in." It's always better to be let in.

CHAPTER 4

Working with People Who Don't Speak English

If you go into a bookstore and scan the titles in the business, relationship or self-improvement sections, you'll see that "communication" is a key topic. *Always*. It never goes away. Twenty years ago, books were written about improving communication skills and twenty years from now, there will *still* be books and articles offering suggestions for better communication. The ongoing popularity of this topic suggests that we all struggle with simply communicating with others, whether it's at work or in our personal relationships.

It's difficult enough to communicate effectively in *one* language, so imagine the challenges that accompany working with people who don't speak the same language that you do, or don't speak it well. Then mix in all the *other* challenges and pressures we face at work, such as conflict resolution, different personalities, management expectations and more, and you've got a recipe for disaster stew.

If you work with people who don't speak English, or don't speak English well, you know firsthand what this is like. It's not only difficult, it can be *exhausting*. It takes more time, energy and focus to communicate with someone who doesn't speak the same language. It can feel burdensome. And it can be stressful, because you may not be sure that you're being fully understood or that you fully understand what the other person is saying.

The restaurant industry has felt the impact of this issue greatly. In the United States, many restaurant workers are from Latin America and most have little or no English proficiency when they arrive in the United States. It takes a long time to learn a new language, so they gravitate to jobs where it's not mandatory to have strong English skills. Many start working in restaurants as cooks, dishwashers, and other "behind the scenes" jobs, such as clearing tables and cleaning. The managers and supervisors of many restaurants often *don't* speak Spanish, so there is a language barrier. How do they function?

Vince is a manager of a Chipotle restaurant in Dallas, Texas. He's a White guy and doesn't speak Spanish—or any language other than

English. Most of his employees are Hispanic. This is partly due to the composition of the local population (more than 40 percent of people who live in Dallas are Hispanic) and partly because the restaurant industry attracts many Hispanic workers. Vince is a great guy and a terrific manager, so his employees refer others to him when there are open positions at the restaurant. When most of your employees are Hispanic and they refer others they know, chances are those others are also Hispanic. So Vince's Hispanic workforce continues to grow with each new referral and addition to the team. On a daily basis, Vince has to manage the operations of his restaurant and communicate with people who don't speak English. Vince says it's not always easy, but here's what he's learned that works:

1. Slow down when you speak. It's really hard to understand another language when the speaker talks fast. I think this is true for any language. Your coworkers who are learning English may know words and key sentences, but when they're spoken quickly, they may not be able to keep up and comprehend what's being said. The words sound blurred together. It's better to slow down and enunciate clearly.

2. Use simple and clear phrases. Vince says it's better to say, "Stop working now; go home" than, "Your shift is up." And "your shift is up" brings up another important issue: slang and use of idioms makes it harder to communicate. In most languages, "up" refers to a direction: "the elevator is going up" or "sales are up." In the example above, "your shift is up," the word "up" means expired. A native speaker of English knows this, but someone learning the language would not. Strive for clarity. For example, "take control of the situation" is a far more clear direction than "take the bull by the horns." Language is full of phrases that don't mean exactly what the words say. I will never forget working with Alvaro Cabal, who is from Colombia. When he moved to the United States, he studied English tirelessly and became fluent within a couple of years. But he always challenged me on phrases I used that he didn't understand. Once we were in a meeting with five others trying to solve a client problem and I said, "there's more than one way to skin a cat." He was horrified. He stopped the meeting right there

and said, "Wait! Why are we talking about killing cats? That's horrible! Why would we do that?" It made us all laugh, but it also pointed out how so much of what we say is idiomatic and doesn't literally mean what the words actually say.

3. Write words down. This may seem counterintuitive, but Vince and others who work with non-English speakers say writing things down can be helpful. Sometimes the worker who doesn't speak English well knows the words when they see them, even if they have trouble pronouncing those words or remembering them in conversation. For simple instruction, writing words down can be useful. Combined with a conversation, writing words down boosts comprehension. Written instruction is also useful if they need to ask a bilingual coworker for clarification.

4. Use pictures, charts, or graphs, or draw a picture if you have to. Even the most rudimentary sketches still convey meaning.

5. Gestures and pantomimes also boost comprehension. An insulation installing company trained their workers who were not fluent in English by doing "show and tell." They would demonstrate how to install the insulation, using simple phrases while doing so. Then the worker would have to do it, demonstrating that they understood how to do the installation. It's a pretty basic approach, but an effective one, and one that can be applied to many roles where the job can be learned by observing someone else do it and then performing it. Vince states, "It's easier than you think to communicate with a combination of hand gestures and language."

6. When possible, make labels or instructions in both languages.

7. Make sure workers know that if they don't understand something *questions are appreciated* and it's important that they understand their job and how to perform it. So often, people are embarrassed or uncomfortable admitting they don't understand what's being said, so what do they do? They smile and nod! It's almost a universal response when someone doesn't understand what another is saying. The nod gives the impression that the person understands, when in fact they don't. Vince said that although he doesn't speak Spanish, he makes it a point to say, "¿Preguntas?" (Questions?) when talking with and training his

staff. The fact that he switches to *their* language for that one word makes them more comfortable in asking questions or asking for help.

8. Use your bilingual employees to assist you. But don't just say, "Hey, tell the other guys _____." Explain that you're going to need their help on an ongoing basis and *reward them for their extra effort*. A raise or tangible gift (like a gift card to a restaurant or store) is best, but if you can't do that, then at least heap praise upon them and thank them often for their help. Chances are they didn't sign up to do their job *and* be a translator. Recognition and appreciation are always valued.

9. Be patient. It can be frustrating to not be able to communicate easily with another person. But losing patience won't help. And if the process is frustrating for you, I assure you the other person feels this and senses your impatience. A smile can help break the tension and make communicating easier.

10. Don't give up! Every day your coworkers who don't speak English will be exposed to more English here and there: at work, the grocery store, at restaurants, on TV. Exposure to language is how we learn. It's how children learn to talk. Little by little, vocabulary grows and so does comprehension. It takes a long time to learn a language. The coworker who struggles with English is doing a job, with all the demands of that job, but with a huge disadvantage. *Yet they're doing it.* They're working, doing their best, despite the significant disadvantage of not being able to express themselves or possibly fully understand what's being discussed around them. Don't avoid them or give up on them. Hang in there and help them.

Now here's what *doesn't* work: talking louder. Simply turning up the volume doesn't snap someone into speaking English (or any other language for that matter). It's understandable why people do it—it's an on-the-spot attempt to connect, but it doesn't work and can be interpreted as rude, aggressive, or just weird.

What about working with people who speak English, but speak with very heavy accents and are difficult to understand? There are two tactics that can help foster communication. The first may seem rather extreme. I've only had to use it a few times myself, but it can be a lifesaver when you simply cannot understand what the other person is saying. The usual response when someone says something you don't understand is to reply, "pardon me?" and the person speaking will repeat what they've said. Most often it's a word that's hard to understand, not an entire sentence. If you still don't understand, you can say politely that you're having difficulty understanding them and could they please repeat it, more slowly. That will usually suffice, but if it doesn't, here is a tactic that will work. However, I recommend this tactic only as a last resort, because it puts a strain on the conversation. When I absolutely cannot understand what someone is saying, no matter how slowly they say it or how often they repeat it, I say, "I'm so sorry, I don't want to keep asking you to repeat yourself. Can you spell it for me?" Saying that politely, respectfully, and with a smile conveys that it's not a put-down, it's a sincere attempt to understand someone. I have never had anyone get mad at the request—they usually laugh and start spelling. It's not the smoothest of techniques, but it works.

The second tactic to use with someone who speaks with a heavy accent is to repeat critical information to sum up a conversation. If you work with someone who speaks your language but you have difficulty understanding them, it's important to be clear about next steps or other specifics that affect you both. It's perfectly fine to wrap up a conversation with a question that confirms what you've heard and understood. For example, you could say, "Okay, so we'll meet again at 3 p.m. Thursday to review the budget forecast but you need the quarterly sales numbers by Wednesday, is that correct?" Confirming that everyone is clear and on the same page is essential, particularly when there is the possibility that someone might be misunderstood due to the way they speak. It's best to confirm your understanding of the conversation and, as long as it's done professionally and respectfully, it should not be an issue.

When you're working with people who don't speak English or don't speak it well, it's easy to get frustrated and impatient. Try not to get hung up on what's lacking in their English. Keep in mind that it's their second (if not third, fourth, or fifth) language. Good communication is the responsibility of everyone involved. Recognize the efforts your coworker has made to learn and use English and help them on this journey.

CHAPTER 5 ➤➤

Dealing with People, Groups, or Values You Don't Like:

How to Get Along and Work Together Anyway

I once worked with a guy who everyone avoided because he was so negative. I don't mean that he was a little gruff or that he was mean. He wasn't—he just saw the glass as "half empty" rather than "half full." Actually, he was so negative that he would have said the glass was half full—of *poison*. If you said, "Good morning, Josh," he'd say something along the lines of, "Well, I hope it will be a good morning, but it probably won't be." Or if you asked, "Hey, Josh, are you ready for the client meeting today?" he'd reply, "I guess. I'm sure they're going to hate all of our concepts and suggestions, but I guess we have to go through the motions." Wow! It didn't exactly make anyone want to grab a cup of coffee with him or ask him about his weekend.

Behind his back, the people in the office called him Eeyore—you know, after the Winnie the Pooh character. Eeyore is pessimistic, dismal, sarcastic, depressed, cynical and perpetually gloomy, and those adjectives described Josh perfectly. Because he was such a downer, people in the office *avoided* him. No one was outright rude or mean to him, but you can tell when people are avoiding you. You can feel when people are shunning you or excluding you. I'm convinced that Josh felt this isolation, which only made him even more negative.

I'm an optimist. I tend to see the world through eyes that are hopeful, and I believe that no matter how bad things get, the sun will rise tomorrow. Josh and I had personalities and views that were polar opposites, but we had to work together. I didn't like working with him because his negative outlook was draining. I'd leave every meeting with him feeling exhausted and depleted and I *resented* that—and him! He was like a vampire—he sucked the energy and fun out of everything.

I kept trying to like him. I felt kind of sorry for him and his gloomy state of mind, and I tried to channel that into empathy, but I wasn't able to. I felt like I had to steel myself for even the shortest meetings with him. I resented the *effort* that went into working with him.

Then one day I had an epiphany: I don't *have* to like him! That's not part of my job! My job was to keep our client's business moving forward. That meant communicating with team members, solving problems, removing obstacles and barriers that stood in the way of implementation and facilitating cooperation and support among the departments. My list of responsibilities did not include "liking Josh."

I didn't have to have dinner with him. I didn't have to hang out with him on weekends. I didn't have to invite him to a backyard barbeque. *I just had to work with him*. And while working with others isn't always easy, the key elements of teamwork are pretty basic: cooperation, respect, trust, support, shared goals, and communication.

When you don't like someone you work with, when they rub you the wrong way or annoy you, when your views clash or your workstyles conflict in significant ways, it's because you have different values. Pinpoint what it is about them that irritates you and you'll learn something about your own values—and where the friction comes from.

My friend Sara was telling me about a woman she works with who constantly interrupts her when they're talking. Sara said, "It's not an occasional thing—it's *constant*! It's so jarring because I was raised to never interrupt anyone. My parents drilled it into my head that interrupting someone is disrespectful, so I am completely uncomfortable every time it happens."

Ahhhhhh: there's the difference in *values*. Yes, interrupting someone is a rude habit, but for Sara, it's more than an issue of etiquette. It's *completely foreign to how she was raised*. Her core values won't permit her to interrupt another person, so she is bewildered by someone who does.

Here's another example, in a different vein: Dale is a hunter. It's his passion. He hunts deer and elk and his lifelong dream was to go on an African safari and hunt big game. He did that and when he returned from his trip, he filled his office with photographs of his excursion and the animals that he had successfully hunted. Those photographs were upsetting to one of his coworkers, Samantha, who volunteers her time working to protect animal rights. Samantha can't comprehend how anyone can look at an animal and pull a trigger. For Dale, it's a sport he takes great pride in and one that he finds challenging and exciting.

Neither Dale nor Samantha is "right" or "wrong"—they just have very different values when it comes to this specific issue. Samantha doesn't have to like hunting and Dale doesn't have to stop hunting. They simply have to acknowledge that this is an area that they don't see eye-to-eye on because of their personal values.

When we come into contact with someone who has different values or beliefs from ours, it can be jarring. Our instinct is usually to prove that we are "right" and they are "wrong." Or, at a minimum, to confirm that our view/way/approach is better.

Having different values creates judgments about the other person and that's what is at the root of that feeling of dislike. You dislike the way they do things or their beliefs or habits. Liking—or disliking—someone is an emotion. That's why it's so stressful to work with someone you dislike—it's *emotionally involving* and makes you feel other unpleasant emotions, like frustration, impatience, anger, resentment, despair, or futility.

When you take the emotion out of it, when you realize and *accept* that you don't have to like them, you just have to work with them, it makes things easier. It's about work, not socializing. It's about cooperation, not friendship. It's about respect, not being soulmates. You don't have to see eye-to-eye on everything, or share the same views: you *just have to get along well enough to get the job done.*

How do you do this? In Chapter 2, I talked about my client Somir and his successful business in Texas. He's from India. He's in the automotive financing industry and some of his clients are hard-partying, hard-drinking, hard-smoking, strongly prejudiced, and opinionated people. Somir is very mild mannered, cultured, and civil, and he doesn't smoke, drink, or party. In other words, many of Somir's clients are "not like him" and at times their words, behavior, or habits can offend. I asked him how he put up with clients like this, how he could stand to do business with people like that, and he said, "It's not about finding what's *wrong* with them. It's about finding our common ground and *what we can do together* to grow our business."

Somir's insight is practical. You're not always going to like the people you work with, and sometimes you may actively *dislike* them. But if you focus on the mechanics of working together to further *business*, you can get along with them and do the job at hand.

What do I mean by the mechanics of working together? There are five principles of working with someone you don't like:

1. **Understand that they're not *trying* to be difficult.** People behave the way they were socialized. Socialization is the sum of how you were raised, the cultural influences you were exposed to, and the family framework or dynamics you experienced. All of us are a product of how we were socialized. You are the product of all the experiences, expectations, and interactions you've had. So is the person at work who is different from you or whom you don't like. They're just behaving the only way they know how to behave. It's not right or wrong, but if it's different from *your* values, it can feel very uncomfortable. But it doesn't mean the other person is trying to provoke you. *They're just being who they are.*

2. **Civility wins.** When you have to work with someone you don't like or who is vastly different from you, understand that *you won't change them.* There's no point in arguing or playing games or trying to persuade them to behave differently. Your best bet is to be civil and diplomatic. Whatever their demeanor is toward you (or the job), remain positive and professional and treat the other person with courtesy. If you maintain your composure and stick to civil exchanges, tension is not likely to escalate. And your blood pressure and sanity will thank you for it.

3. **Adjust your expectations.** We often expect others to act as we would or say the things that we would, because that's the only way we can imagine handling a situation. It goes back to how you were socialized. You behave in certain ways because of your upbringing. *So does everyone else!* Our different backgrounds don't always align, so if you expect others to act as you would, you're likely to be disappointed or frustrated. If a coworker always does something that irritates you or you know that you have vastly different viewpoints, don't expect their behavior or their opinions to mesh with yours. Adjust your expectations—accept that the other person is a certain way and they'll be less likely to push your buttons.

4. **Don't veer from "the business of business."** You're there to do a job and so are they. Successful work relationships don't have to be rooted in liking each other. It sure is a plus when you *do* like your

coworkers, but success on the job is about cooperation, respect, solving problems, and working together for a positive outcome. Focus on the outcome you're seeking and what you and your coworkers need to do to get there.

5. **Agree to disagree.** You don't have to suppress your opinions or meekly go along with conversations in which your views or values differ from a coworker's. There's a professional way to state your views without being antagonistic or trying to persuade the other person to shift their view. Say, "I see it differently" and then express your view on whatever subject is being discussed. "I see it differently" is nonjudgmental: it doesn't come across as combative, it doesn't mean you're trying to "win the argument" or persuade the other person to change their opinion. It is a simple, declarative statement that allows you to express a different point of view without coming across as if your view is superior. It diffuses tension and can lead to constructive conversation that allows you and your coworker to work together more peacefully and productively.

Does it feel like this is all on you? In other words, why should you be the only one putting in the effort to get along with someone you don't like or agree with or someone whose values are completely different or distasteful to you? It would be nice if your coworkers were striving for harmony as you are, but you can't expect that. What you *can* expect is that if you follow the five principles above, you and your coworkers will be able to work together productively. And that's the objective, the *goal that matters when it comes to work.*

PART II ➤➤

Leading People Not Like You—How to Get a Diverse Group of People to Trust Each Other and Work Together

CHAPTER 6 ⯈
How to Break the Ice and Build Trust in Diverse Work Groups

As a leader, your role is to bring groups of people together to generate the greatest possible productivity and best outcome for your company and customers. That can take many forms: innovation, greater efficiency, greater output or production, new products or services, greater profitability, enhanced customer loyalty and retention, employee engagement, and more.

Study after study shows that working with diverse groups of people leads to *all of the above*. Why? Because teams of people who are largely the same usually have the same backgrounds, same mindsets, same experiences. They view things through the same lens of life. Consequently, they tend to think alike and aren't as creative when it comes to innovation or developing new solutions to problems.

Teams of people with diverse backgrounds and experience bring new ideas, new perspectives, and different ways of viewing issues. This fosters better thinking, which leads to better idea generation and more innovative problem solving. It's proven. It has a real, measurable effect on the bottom line as well, such as greater sales and profits or greater value of a company's stock.

As a leader, you probably know all of this. You have been entrusted with moving your business forward, with the team or teams you oversee. Your company believes that you possess the skills that will drive success.

Leadership is tough—that's why there are so many books and courses and webinars and schools of thought on leadership styles and what works or doesn't work. You probably know firsthand how difficult it can be to lead teams of people who are largely the same. And now you're faced with leading a group of people who are *not the same* as one another. The challenges and pressure that this responsibility brings are enormous. You're expected to lead people who may not be anything alike. They may have different backgrounds and cultures, be of different races or ethnicities, speak different languages, be of different genders or generations, have different personalities, different levels of education or experience, work in different time zones, or be scattered all over the world.

It's a daunting role and responsibility. All eyes are upon you: those of your team, of course, but also your management's, as well as the rest of the company. You were given this position of leadership because you're the best person for the job. You want to succeed at this, but you don't know how to begin.

START HERE

There are two things that must happen before you can lead your diverse team. You can't "share the vision" or discuss innovation or solutions until these two things happen. In fact, nothing productive will happen—nothing *can* happen—with a diverse team without these two fundamental steps. You can't skip them. They are essential.

Step One: Breaking the ice with diverse team members
Step Two: Building trust

These two steps are also sequential—you must do them in order. You have to break the ice before you can begin building trust among people.

HOW TO BREAK THE ICE WITH DIVERSE TEAM MEMBERS

The best way to break the ice is to get people talking in safe, easy ways. Starting with easy discussion topics is an effective tactic because it puts people at ease and they start to see each other as individuals, rather than stereotypes. As a leader, you want to foster conversation among your team so that they get comfortable with *each other* so that they'll ultimately become comfortable with talking about issues. This is important because diverse team members usually want to have conversations about diversity, but aren't sure how their statements or questions might be interpreted, so they tend to be extra cautious or say nothing at all. How can they troubleshoot or solve a complex problem down the road if they can't comfortably talk to one another?

To break the ice and get your group talking to each other, start by holding a meeting where the stated objective is two-fold:

1. To make sure that everyone on the team knows each other
2. To begin ongoing discussions about how the team will work together

Your team can't be effective if they don't know who's who—they'll need to know who to turn to with questions or difficulties and what the preferred channels of communication are.

When you pull your team together for the first time, for the meeting to break the ice, here are key dos and don'ts that will help to plant the seeds of trust among them:

- *Don't* single people out. Don't call on people individually and have them report their name, department and area of responsibility. While that information is important, it's not the best way to break the ice. It's impersonal and corporate-y and pretty boring, too.
- *Do* ask each person to share something about themselves, but have them jot it down, instead of reciting it. Good questions to ask team members are those that ask them to share something personal about themselves, but that are also safe and neutral. Here are some good ones to try:
  - Where do you call home?
  - What's one thing you're grateful for this week?
  - A perfect Saturday for you would be...

  An exercise like this helps team members *relate to each other.* (After all, everyone has a home or feels gratitude or can construct what a perfect Saturday would look like.) Sharing something personal helps create trust and helps your team see one another as individuals. They see what other team members are really like, not what they might have *thought* they'd be like. I'll never forget when I went through this kind of exercise at a large company I worked for. The leader asked each person to share something that no one in the group was likely to know about them. A guy from the accounting department with whom I'd never spoken before and didn't know at all shared that he and his wife were in the process of adopting a little girl. Of course, everyone in the room said, "Awwwwww, that's so great." But it was more than just a touching moment: it became a topic that he and I talked about every time we met thereafter. *This little personal insight about him made me* want *to get to know him better, because it revealed something about him as a person, not an accountant.* It was a human touchpoint that allowed us to connect in a meaningful way, but also *served as a springboard into other conversations.* I would ask about his daughter, but eventually we'd also get around to talking about business. We developed trust over time. I saw him as a capable accountant, but also as a doting dad. He saw me as a colleague who always made a point of asking about his little girl. It made us want to work with each other because we saw the "real" in each other, not just our job titles.

- *Don't* ask people to share their answers one at a time in front of the group. That can be intimidating. Try pairing them up to share and discuss their answers. If they don't already know each other, they will introduce themselves and start talking. I promise this is where you'll hear laughter and your team will relax into normal conversation. Let this happen and give them time to enjoy themselves.

- *Do* have each pair report back to the larger group for a fuller discussion. Open it up to Q&A. Let the conversation take a natural course. For example, one pair might share that Laura is from Cincinnati originally. Another person might jump in with, "Cincinnati? That's where Graeters Ice Cream is headquartered! Have you ever had their ice cream? It's the best on the planet!" Or, "My friend Jamie lives in Cincy—he says the winters there are long and gray—is that true?"

LEADING A VIRTUAL TEAM

What if you're leading a virtual team? A team that may never have met each other—and may not ever meet face-to-face? Breaking the ice is just as important—maybe more so—in these circumstances. You can still go through the exercise of everyone sharing something about themselves, but in a different way. Instead of pairing people up, hold a virtual meeting and have each person share some of their background expertise, coupled with one personal fact or insight that others aren't likely to know. Another idea is to create a team website and have everyone write a paragraph or two about themselves. And here's an idea I love: one leader of a team asked his people to share one work highlight—for example, something they loved working on or an assignment where they learned something new—and one "trick" that they knew how to do. Everyone knows how to do some kind of trick! One woman said she knows how to do a formal English curtsy; one guy said he can recite every state capitol in the United States backwards—you get the idea. When they shared their tricks, many of which were pretty random, childish or bizarre, the group laughed for an hour. Imagine how fun it could be to work with people knowing that they can do some weird trick? What a great idea for an ice-breaker conversation.

With a virtual team, it's important to set the standard that they must treat each other just as if they were working face-to-face. That means being on time for conference calls or virtual meetings or letting each other know when they'll be unavailable or on vacation.

Whether your team is in the same office or workplace as you or across the world, you've got to get them talking to each other. Once you do that, you're able to start the process of building trust.

BUILDING TRUST

Having trust in team members is critical to any high-performing team. A team cannot function effectively without it. But it's not like you can wave a magic wand and—POOF!— people trust each other. Trust is built bit by bit, over time. Our experiences with others reveals whether we can trust them: how they handle problems or conflict, whether they share information or hoard it, whether they work to advance the team or to advance their own agenda, whether they admit mistakes and learn from them or blame others. All of these behaviors and more clue us in as to whether we can trust someone at work.

Psychologists say there are two kinds of trust: "common trust" and "vulnerability trust." Common trust is what we extend to others pretty broadly, even if we don't know them. For example, we trust that when we drive a car, other drivers will follow the rules of the road and not run red lights or drive on the wrong side of the road. Or if we fly, we trust that the pilot will get us safely to our destination. At work, common trust is usually extended to team members automatically. We assume that if you are on the team, you must be competent.

Vulnerability is trust that must be cultivated. Vulnerability trust means that you have confidence in your team members, enough to be *vulnerable*. It means you feel safe with your team members, safe enough to allow you to take risks, ask for help, and admit mistakes. Safe enough that you can confront and hold others accountable without fear of retaliation or resentment.

This type of trust is not granted automatically. It's earned over time. And it is both earned *and* given. If one person on a team trusts another, but the trust is not reciprocated, that team will never reach its full potential. Strong, high-performing teams base their entire foundation on vulnerability trust.

You can't "make" people trust each other. But you can foster the growth of trust among your team members. Here are ten ways that leaders work with their teams to build vulnerability trust:

1. Go first. As a leader, it's up to you to lead by example and show others the type of behavior and actions you want them to adopt. Do this by "going first" when it comes to opening up and sharing something that makes you vulnerable with your team. For example, if you're newly promoted into your position, you could say, "I've been given this responsibility, but I've never done this before, so I am sure I will make mistakes along the way. But I promise to be honest with you about my mistakes and work through them with you to learn from them and be better."

2. Listen. This is harder to do than you may think. In business, we are conditioned to contribute and to compete. But leading an effective team is not a competition. You don't have to "win." Your job is to lead and you can't do that if you don't listen to what your team is telling you. You must be willing to suspend your own competitive thoughts and open up to considering someone else's idea. Experts say the goal is to listen with the intent to *understand* rather than with the intent to *reply*.

3. Talk straight. Be honest. Tell the truth, *even when it's difficult truth*. People can handle the truth—what they can't handle is the runaround or being left to figure out what's really going on.

4. Use simple language. I vividly remember sitting in a meeting with Toyota executives and the vice president of sales saying, "We can't hit our sales numbers unless we hit our truck numbers." It was a simple statement, but illuminated a *clear objective*: increase truck sales.

5. Be clear about expectations. Your team can't deliver on what you expect if they're unsure of what the expectations are. Don't make them guess or wonder. Don't pussyfoot around it. State your expectations and use the opportunity to clarify any questions or issues around the subject. The president of Itron, a global provider of meters for the utility industry, told me about their deadline for creating and manufacturing a new product. It had to be in the market by a certain date. The development team balked, saying it would be impossible to meet the deadline. The president stated that it had to happen—*they had to find a way*. It wasn't popular news, but the entire team clearly understood what the deadline was. And they delivered. Clarity builds trust, because with clarity, people *have the same understanding of what is needed to do the job*.

6. Demonstrate respect. Show you care. I worked with the Department of Defense on a project and my client told me about all the different types of people who work there: ex-military professionals, civilian executives, scientists, multilingual associates, you name it. Very diverse teams of people, all working with one shared mission: keep the United States safe. The Department of Defense has many super-brains working there, people who are smarter than anyone you've ever met in your life. They're not normal—they're truly geniuses. They crack codes, for crying out loud! Many are high-functioning autistic, with Asperger's Syndrome, which makes them able to focus intently on one thing for extended periods of time. My client told me that, more than once, she has had to tell one of the super-brain workers on her team to go home, eat something, get some sleep, take a shower, and change their shirt. I chuckled when she said that, and commented that it must be difficult to tell a coworker that they smell! But she said, "You don't understand—these guys get so caught up in what they're working on, they can be so singularly focused, that they lose track of time. For *days*. They'll stay here

for days. They don't go home. They forget to eat. They don't sleep. I *worry* about them! I have to tell them to go home and get some sleep and a shower." She demonstrates to her team members that *she cares about them*. Her request for them to go home and grab a shower may be triggered by the fact that she can smell them, but it's rooted in *care*. She worries about them when they work like maniacs. She respects these guys. And she shows this respect to them by insisting that they take a break and take care of themselves. When you, as a leader, demonstrate respect and care for your people, they will respect each other and look out for one another.

7. Right wrongs. The ability to admit mistakes and show personal humility is a strength. When you mess up, it's important to apologize and make things right. It shows your team you won't blame others or let your personal pride get in the way of doing the right thing. It fosters trust because it shows them that, while you may not be perfect, you will take responsibility.

8. Follow through. Keep your promises and commitments. Following through builds trust quickly, because team members will realize that you do what you say you're going to do. *They'll learn they can depend on you.* Modeling this sets the standard for the rest of the team: if you can follow through on your commitments, so can they. If you've made a promise and something happens that prohibits you from fulfilling that commitment, say so. Tell your team up front, and do it right away. Don't let them hear it through the grapevine. They need to hear it from you so they can ask questions or express themselves. For example, saying, "I know this is what we discussed and what I said I could do. There's been a change and we won't be able to go forward with that. I'm as disappointed as you are," lets them know what the situation is—truthfully. It is also an opportunity to acknowledge emotions, such as frustration or disappointment. If you are leading a virtual team, your follow through is crucial. Your word and your follow through may be the only thing you can give people who you may never meet in person.

9. Show loyalty. You trust your loyal friends, right? It's the same with a leader or a team. Loyalty is a cherished characteristic and it's often lacking in the corporate world. When you show

loyalty to your team, when you stand up for them, when you give credit where it's due, when you keep team members' personal information private, trust is formed. Don't badmouth the company. Don't badmouth people behind their backs—that will erode trust faster than anything. Stephen R. Covey, a master at leadership and building trust within teams, said, "*If you want to retain those who are present, be loyal to those who are absent.*"

10. Allow for differences. A team may be a singular entity, but it's comprised of different people. Your diverse team may have very different views on the right approach, the right behaviors, the right way to resolve conflict. For example, some on a team may feel that expressing emotion is inappropriate in the workplace, whereas others may feel that open and honest expression of feelings is the basis for a solid working relationship. Some may feel that the leader of the team should make a final decision when a difference of opinion exists, whereas others may believe that consensus is needed or "majority rules." As the leader of a diverse team, understand that differences will *always* exist and allow for those differences to be discussed and dissected. Show that you consider all opinions and views valid. Don't squash someone's view just because it differs from yours or the team's view. Demonstrating that you value the diversity of the team shows your team the core strength that they possess.

Building trust takes time, but it happens in teams when respect, cooperation, listening, caring, and integrity are at the very foundation of the team. Model the behavior and attitude you want your team to have and they will follow your lead.

CHAPTER 7 ➤➤
The Leader's Role: Educating and Setting the Example

How would you handle it if one of the top executives in your company told you they are transitioning to another gender? I'm betting that might really throw you. It's one of the most challenging and difficult diversity issues an organization can face. It would also truly put your "we value diversity" mantra to the test, because you'd have to explain it to your other associates and ensure the news was handled with sensitivity and respect.

This is exactly what a large Southern law firm was faced with recently. Their chief learning officer (CLO) came out as a transgender woman. She'd been living and presenting as a man who then transitioned to living authentically as a woman. That's not a diversity issue that many firms have much experience with. It's different from other aspects of employee diversity—after all, no one asks an Asian person why they are Asian or asks a person who uses a wheelchair why they don't walk. Transgender identity is difficult for many people to understand and grasp. This law firm needed to tell their associates that Bob was becoming Sarah. This firm had a stated commitment to diversity and their handling of this news would be the true test of the respect and inclusion they espoused to their hundreds of associates. While most readers aren't going to face this particular issue, the way it was handled applies to any challenge that leaders face around "leading people not like you." Here's how they did it.

- Lead by Example
  Bob was the CLO, and worked closely with the leadership of the law firm. Bob informed the top executives of his need to undertake gender transition and together they made a plan for sharing the news with the more than 600 associates at the firm. They knew the news would come as a shock to many. They also knew that all eyes would be upon them and that what they said, did, and expected of their associates would be watched closely by all. They had to lead by example.

- The CEO sent a memo to all associates. There is no way I can adequately summarize how perfect this memo was, so here is the actual text:

> *Dear _____.*
>
> *A valued firm employee, Bob Smith, has for some time been undergoing medical, social and legal changes related to a long-standing medical condition known as Gender Dysphoria (popularly called transgenderism or transsexualism). Although these changes have been mostly private so far, the next stage in this process involves all of us.*
>
> *On March 17, our colleague will begin working full-time in her appropriate female gender role and thereafter will be known, both at the firm and otherwise, as Sarah Smith. Sarah is fortunate to have the support, understanding and guidance of her health-care providers, family and friends throughout her gender transition process, and she has been reassured by us that she has this firm's support as well. In keeping with our efforts to accommodate Sarah in her need to live and work in her appropriate gender role, we are asking for your help in facilitating any adjustments that may be required to implement this personal change.*
>
> *While the firm has a long history of supporting diversity in the workplace, we do recognize the potential for questions this change might raise. As always, our goal is to ensure an environment in which employees of diverse backgrounds and beliefs feel welcome and can work free of harassment, intimidation or discrimination. We are attaching our Equal Employment Opportunity Policy, which expressly prohibits discrimination or harassment based on gender identity. We expect each of you will continue to support Sarah in the performance of her job.*
>
> *It is Sarah's wish and desire that this process be carried out in a private, dignified and respectful manner to*

minimize any disruption that may occur. While some people at the firm already know about Sarah's transition, and pledged their support, we anticipate that a variety of personal reactions will surface as this change occurs.

To help address questions and concerns, and to explain the firm's expectations with respect to this change, we have arranged for Mary Jones (an employment attorney) to present a training and information session. Pertinent literature and other reading material will be made available. Further, Sarah's personal letter to everyone accompanies this letter.

The firm is working to support Sarah during this transition period and asks that you do the same. Your understanding and cooperation are much appreciated.

Signed by the CEO

What a wonderful opportunity to model the firm's core values! The announcement was professional, supportive and sincere. The CEO's letter addressed Sarah's change directly, truthfully, and respectfully. This is important for leaders to do, because if you pussyfoot around issues or disguise them by using language that is not clear or factual, it conveys that you are uncomfortable. *You can't effectively lead a diverse team if you are uncomfortable with your own people.* Truth breeds trust. If you are truthful with your team, they will trust you to lead them.

- Foster Safe Discussion of Issues
  Another step that this law firm took that was impressive was they anticipated the questions they would get from the associates and they prepared accordingly. In addition to having the employment attorney conduct a training and information session, they also had Sarah's gender therapist join the session. Her role was to answer questions from the staff that were not about legal issues surrounding Sarah's change. They wanted to know why and how and a million other questions. The law firm anticipated that there would be a myriad of questions, both legal and personal, and they created a forum for open discussion. The result was that

people didn't need to talk about Sarah or whisper about her in the hallways—they had a chance to talk about her change—and their feelings about it—safely and with professional guidance. As a leader, you may not have to navigate waters that are as complex as the one this law firm went through, but you should strive to foster safe discussion of issues.

Good leaders know that it's not only okay to discuss issues, even tough ones, but that it's important to do so. When we discuss issues, we learn that there are diverse perspectives in business. Discovering diverse perspectives is imperative, because without them, we *might miss something big*. Here's an example.

Have you heard of, or had, a Skinnygirl cocktail? If you're a woman, I am betting the answer is yes. If you're a man, you may be familiar with the brand, but thinking, "so what?" Skinnygirl is a line of premixed cocktails that are much lower in calories and carbs than most cocktails. It's an innovative product and has been tremendously successful. What I like most about it though is the back story on its creation—what happened behind the scenes when Skinnygirl's creator, Bethany Frankel, was trying to launch the product and the brand. Or maybe I should say, what *didn't* happen.

Bethany Frankel approached all the major liquor companies with her idea for Skinnygirl cocktails. Every one of them dismissed her product. That turned out to be a bad decision. She forged ahead on her own, developed the brand, and sold more than 2 million bottles in her first year in business. Two years later, Beam, the makers of bourbon and other liquors, acquired the product and brand for an estimated $100 million. Yes—*$100 million*. Skinnygirl sales continued to skyrocket: in its first year as a Beam product, Skinnygirl posted a whopping 486 percent in net sales growth.

Beam was smart enough to acquire Skinnygirl. But initially, they and all the other major liquor companies dismissed the brand and the concept. Why? At the time, all the major liquor companies were led by men. I may be going out on a limb here, but I am betting they all passed on Skinnygirl because *they didn't see the need for it*. Men typically aren't as calorie-conscious as women. It's likely they just couldn't relate to the product. They underestimated—or completely dismissed—the demand for this product. They had no idea women would find this product to be an *answered prayer*. The women

I know would kill to be able to enjoy a cocktail or two and not blow 20 percent of their day's allotted calories! The men at the large liquor companies simply couldn't relate—so they passed on the opportunity. It was a failure of *perspective*: they failed to see value in the product because they had no idea how women would respond to it. Oops!

We all do this. It's human nature. We devalue, undervalue, or dismiss the things we can't relate to or see no need for. That's why *it's so important to have diverse perspectives in business. If we don't, we might miss something big.*

Diversity is good for business. Forbes, Gallup, and dozens of other research organizations have studied companies with diverse teams, as well as those without, and the findings are clear: across every metric, diverse teams yield better results. Better sales, larger market share, faster growth, more innovation, greater profits, better employee tenure, and engagement. It's a no-brainer. Diverse teams deliver what companies want today. So why is it still so hard? Why do companies and organizations struggle with diversity? With irrefutable data supporting the *business value of diversity,* you'd think executives would be racing to build organizations that are as diverse as they can possibly be. It's happening, but not as quickly—or as broadly—as you'd think. Why?

I think it's because, while many organizations value diversity, they don't know how to fully embrace it. They hire a few women or people of color, or they're gay-friendly, so they think they can "check diversity off the list." But companies that truly invest in making their organizations diverse, the ones that are not only successful, but also drive innovation with blockbuster ideas and growth, they *breathe* diversity. It's a function of their corporate body and, like breathing, it keeps them alive.

MAKING "WE VALUE DIVERSITY" REAL FOR YOUR PEOPLE

What do good leaders do to make diversity effective? Three things:

1. They walk the walk.
2. They educate their people about diversity: *on an ongoing basis.*
3. They make a diversity plan and treat it like any other business plan.

Walking the Walk

Diversity isn't a fad nor is it a gimmick. It's an integral, valued approach to doing business. You can't just throw a diversity slogan up on the wall and call it a day. It must be practiced and cultivated every day. Most important, it must be *modeled*. As a leader, your team looks to you to set the standard for how you work. Associates can tell when a leader or a company is sincere. They can also tell when something is just being given lip service.

Consider this: a PwC survey showed that a company's policy on diversity and equality was high on associates' lists when considering whether to work for an organization. But they often felt let down: a whopping 70 percent said that, while their employer talked a good story on diversity, in reality, opportunities weren't equal for all. Here are things you can do that demonstrate that you *sincerely* value diversity:

- Get support from the top or _be_ the support at the top. As CEO of Kaiser Permanente, George Halverson walked the walk. He personally rode in a float for San Francisco's Gay Pride Week. Although Kaiser employees and physicians have participated in the parade for years, the fact that the CEO was there, riding in a float, made a strong statement of support. Kaiser Permanente walks the walk: their 14-member board of directors is 50 percent people of color and 36 percent women. Similarly GE, each business unit has a dedicated diversity leader. There are also seven affinity networks (African American, women's, LGBTQ, Hispanic, Asian, veterans and people with disabilities) and each has an executive who reports *directly* to the chairman and CEO. Additionally, GE's top executives review retention of diverse talent in their quarterly meetings. These types of actions and consistent steps let employees know that diversity is taken seriously and is a priority, not a PR tactic

- Have visible role models at all levels of the organization or team—this signals that professional progression is possible. At a conference for young insurance agents (agents under the age of 35), one woman told me she almost didn't go to work for a particular company because she "didn't see anyone at the top who looked like me. I didn't know if I could actually get ahead in an organization like that." She joined the firm anyway, and shortly afterward the company promoted a woman to president. The young agent said, "That was so inspiring to me! It showed me that if she could do it, so could I." You want your employees engaged and inspired and sometimes all it takes to light that fire is knowing that success is possible and reachable

- Prepare the pipeline. Top executives and leaders say they are concerned about talent, skills, and being able to find, recruit, and keep the best employees. Work to fill the pipeline of diverse talent, whether that's doing outreach at local schools (grade school, high school, and college level), providing scholarships or tuition assistance for underserved candidates, offering internships and summer jobs to disadvantaged youth, or offering ongoing management and leadership training to associates

- Make diversity everyone's job. At Bank of America, managers and leaders are expected to grow the bank's diverse workforce. They receive training and resources on an ongoing basis to do this. It is not the HR department's job—it's every leader's job to make sure that associates understand what it takes to achieve their career goals. Their bonuses depend on it.

Educate Your People. Then Repeat. And Repeat. And Repeat...

Diversity is a complex topic. It doesn't come naturally to most people to explore others' perspectives, cultures, viewpoints, or experiences. Leaders have learned that effective diversity efforts must start with education—you have to talk to your team and educate them about why diversity is important and also how their own perspective or "lens" shapes their impressions, perceptions, and opinions. Geri Thomas, chief diversity officer at Bank of America, states, "We unconsciously look to people who agree with us and share our common interests. As leaders, we have to acknowledge unconscious biases. Leaders must encourage everyone to engage in the same priorities, but in their own unique way." (from *Diversity MBA Magazine*) Educating your team isn't just about pushing information toward them; it's also about listening to their feedback and answering their questions.

It's imperative to *keep* educating your group. If you've ever been part of a sales organization, you probably know that companies spend a fortune on sales training. It's an ongoing, continuous process. It's never simply, "Okay, you're trained! Go out and do your stuff and we'll evaluate your work at the end of the year." No, companies spend and invest time and money in *continuous* sales training. Why? Because people forget! They lose sight of the big picture. Sometimes they lose sight of the fundamentals and start taking shortcuts. Sales organizations know that the key to success is *continuous reinforcement of fundamentals*. Sales professionals aren't always learning something new—sometimes they're just having the basics refreshed and reinforced. Companies do this *because it works*. It's the same with educating your team about diversity and how to constructively develop it. You can't assume that you can have one meeting on diversity and "they've got it." You'll need to continuously reinforce and refresh the basics, as well as troubleshoot problems or issues, answer questions, and educate new team members. The great thing about this step is that it reinforces that you "walk the walk." What better way to demonstrate that you sincerely and wholeheartedly value your diverse team's contributions and backgrounds than by consistently putting the topic on the table for discussion?

Make a Diversity Plan and Treat It Like Any Other Business Plan

You wouldn't launch an advertising campaign without a marketing plan. You wouldn't just randomly spend corporate money without a budget plan. You wouldn't turn in a sales forecast without having a plan in place for how to achieve those sales goals. Every aspect of a successful business, company, or team has a plan behind it that drives its direction. It's a roadmap. Without a roadmap, you're just driving around. Without a business plan, you're just working. If you want to cultivate the best diverse team, or bring out the best *within* your diverse team, you need to make a plan for how you'll do that. There are lots of books and resources online on this subject, but here are the basics that comprise virtually all successful diversity plans:

- Get buy-in and support from top management. If you *are* top management, you're off to a great start.
- Build your core team. You'll need to have others help you in leading this and supporting this. Identify the people who will embrace

this effort and can represent diversity in any of its many forms (including diversity of thought). Discuss the issues that may arise and prepare to respond to questions.

- Have the core team work to develop a launch and maintenance strategy.
  - Launch strategies usually include kickoff meetings where everyone hears the same information at the same time as well as what they can expect going forward. For example, will the team receive regular updates on progress? Will there be opportunity to openly discuss diversity issues? Who do they go to with their questions?
  - Maintenance strategies typically include fostering the efforts that yield results. For example, if your goal is to bring more diverse talent into your hiring and development pipeline, then you'll need to focus on outreach and recruiting efforts. And not just once a year at graduation time. You'll need a plan that keeps you visible in diverse communities and lets people know that you're always looking for talented people. You may even have to "grow your own" talent. On a large scale, the tech community is doing just that with "Girls Who Code," an organization dedicated to closing the gender gap in tech by teaching grade school and high school girls how to code. On a small scale, a privately owned, 20-person company that installs insulation in California created their own outreach program to find new talent. They approached local high schools and asked to meet with smart, ambitious seniors who would be graduating in the next year, but who would likely not be going to college. If you don't go into the armed forces or go to college after graduating from high school, where do you go? You go to work. This company wanted to make high school seniors aware of the exceptional, high-paying jobs that were available to them with *no experience necessary*. It was a brilliant strategy. A graduating high school senior can't choose to work in the insulation industry if he or she isn't aware of the industry in the first place, let alone its professional opportunities. This company created a maintenance strategy that ensured they'd have a diverse pool of talent for years to come. A maintenance strategy may also include professional development plans for associates, as well as ongoing training

As a leader, making diversity efforts meaningful for your team or organization is your responsibility. The steps above—walking the walk, educating your team, and making a diversity plan—are essential to making diversity effective and *real*.

DOS AND DON'TS FOR LEADING PEOPLE NOT LIKE YOU

Keep your ear to the ground. Talk to your team, formally and informally. Listen to the "hallway chatter." You know the kind: you overhear an associate talking to another, saying something like, "I don't understand why we're doing this. What does it accomplish, besides being politically correct?" Or, "I guess I'm on the diversity team because I'm the only Black/woman/gay person/disabled/Asian/Hispanic/vet/Muslim here." When you hear hallway chatter like this, it's a clear signal of what you need to address, clarify or explain. Many times, people will say things informally, in "the hallways," that they won't voice in a meeting. These unfiltered conversations are valuable because they can point you to the areas you need to discuss more thoroughly with your team.

There's another way to keep your ear to the ground, to stay plugged in to what your team is thinking or feeling. It's cultivating your "pilot fish." Pilot fish refers to the fish at the front of a school of fish—the pilot fish is the one that changes direction and all the other fish follow. With people, the phrase applies to those individuals who are influential. They're opinion leaders, the one that others look up to. They are informal "leaders" because others follow them—and often confide in them. They may not even know they are pilot fish, but what they say or do influences others in their sphere. Think about your team and who your "pilot fish" are. Then cultivate an ongoing conversation with them about "what they're hearing" or "what they think others are thinking or feeling." You're not asking them to tattle on anyone or name names. Your goal is simply to learn what your team may not be comfortable talking about in a meeting. As a leader, you can't fix problems you're not aware of. You can address an issue if you know it exists—and that's where insight from your pilot fish can help. Here's an example of how a pilot fish can be of tremendous value.

- I was speaking at an event for the U.S. Chamber of Commerce. One of their executives shared with me that in most local chambers only 20 percent of members are active, such as attending meetings or volunteering to be on committees. Just 20 percent! The remaining 80 percent of members drifted in to a meeting here or there, but they weren't fully engaged. Imagine how much more robust and powerful a local chamber could be if they had 80 percent more involvement—80 percent more horsepower, if you will. I asked the executive if they knew why 80 percent were inactive. He said yes: the chamber examined their list of members who were inactive and identified those they felt were influential and may have insight into why attendance at events was spotty. The chamber contacted these "pilot fish" and asked for their help in determining what they could do better to drive attendance and foster better member engagement. The chamber executive shared with me that, through the pilot fish, they learned that younger members felt the chamber events were "stuffy" and "kind of old school" and everyone attending was wearing suits and ties. The pilot fish said, "Young people don't wear suits and ties. And they want to have a voice in how events are planned and how the content is chosen and shared. They want to be involved, but when they go to events, they feel they are just passively listening—they're not able to contribute." Wow! What great insight to have! The issues were completely "fixable"! The chamber worked to create a panel of young executives who suggested topics, themes, and content for meetings. They made the events more casual and social, with lots of networking and informal conversation time baked into the agenda. Not only did younger executives start attending the events, they started bringing friends and colleagues along, thereby expanding membership and involvement in the chamber. It was a major success for the chamber. But the only way they learned what the roadblocks were was by *talking to a pilot fish or two*. You can't fix what you don't know is broken. You'll need help to stay abreast of what your team is thinking, what they're apprehensive about, excited about, or confused about. Your pilot fish are your allies—identify who your pilot fish are and have a sincere conversation with them. It can be as simple as saying, "Debbie, you're a valued associate and people look up to you. As we go through the next six months and work on our diversity plans, I'd love to know what you think might be holding us back or keeping us from being fully effective. Whether it's your own input or what you hear from others, you have a great sense of what's going on with the team and I want your help in identifying what's working and what's not." I have never seen this strategy fail. It works because:

- Your pilot fish are flattered to be asked for their input.
- You get the inside track on what's really on the hearts and minds of your team.
- You identify areas that need your attention that you otherwise might not know of.

Don't "Launch and Abandon"

Nothing will destroy your credibility as a leader faster than launching a new initiative, only to abandon it when things get difficult. The programs and paths that you and your team create are developed because they are important. When things get hard, don't falter. Do what the law firm did and double down on your efforts. It instills credibility and legitimacy in your work. And your team will never forget how you handle difficult situations. In the case of Sarah, the transgender woman at the law firm, one associate at the firm stated, "I was so, so proud of how the firm handled Sarah's transition. We'd always talked about diversity, but the way they handled it was exemplary. It made me appreciate the top execs at the firm. They set the bar high and then raised it."

Celebrate Success

Your diverse team will work through difficult moments, tough issues, conflicting points of view, and disagreements. It's part of diversity. We don't all see things the same way. When your team tackles the tough issues and resolves problems and finds solutions together, celebrate their success. Acknowledge their hard work. Tell them that opinions and approaches don't always align and that that's what makes working together both difficult and rewarding. Give them credit for their efforts and *celebrate how those efforts pay off.*

Set New Goals and Strategies to Strengthen Your Ongoing Efforts

You're never going to be able to "check diversity off the list." It's not a "to do" item. It's ongoing and it will evolve as you and your team evolves. The baby steps you take in the beginning will seem small in hindsight. You'll learn more. You'll get better and smarter. Don't be afraid to refine your efforts and tweak your approaches. Keep the lines of communication open with your team to get their feedback. Create a culture where associates can speak up, contribute solutions, propose ideas that may be novel or irregular or wild, express contrarian opinions, and disagree.

Speaking of contrarian opinions and disagreements, the next chapter will tackle those and how to deal with conflict and prejudice in your team.

CHAPTER 8 ➤➤
Dealing with Conflict and Prejudice and Having Hard Conversations about Differences

When you're working with a diverse group of people, if it feels like the whole process is harder, you're not crazy. It *is* harder. Working with people who are not like you requires more effort. The extra effort feels like it's slowing progress or bogging down productivity. Or it feels like there is tension within the group. There may be real differences between your team members and, sometimes, those differences erupt into conflict. As a leader, how do you deal with conflict, prejudice and real differences between people on your team? How do you drive the best outcome and make your team achieve better results *in spite of their differences?*

DON'T SHY AWAY FROM CONSTRUCTIVE CONFLICT

From the time we are little kids, we're conditioned to play nicely with others. We are told that when someone wants to fight with us, we should walk away—or give in. We are schooled on how to get along with other kids and what not to do. In business, however, you can't just walk away or "give in" whenever you're faced with a difficult situation. You have no choice but to deal with it. The best leaders deal with tough issues head-on. They don't dance around the problem or wait for it to resolve itself or go away. They talk about it. They get the issues on the table and discuss it, no matter how uncomfortable it is. The process can feel awkward, because it's not how we are socialized and brought up, but it's necessary. People think talking about differences between them may make the other person feel uncomfortable, but it actually validates them. It's not disrespectful—it's quite the opposite. It demonstrates tremendous respect to say, "I think we are approaching this in different ways and with different reasons. I want to know how you see things and hear your views." Let me give you an example.

Jay and Dawn are friends of mine who met and fell in love at work. Jay is Jewish and Dawn is Christian. They're both pretty devout and their respective faiths are a key part of their lives. Their parents are even more devout and observant than they are. When they first started dating, their different faiths didn't pose much of an issue. They were just dating and having fun. But as they fell in love and became more serious about each other, they had to discuss their faith. They wanted to get married and start a family. They wanted to build a life together, but they had to have *real* conversations about what that life would be like. Would they raise their children Jewish or Christian? Would they observe Christmas or Hanukkah? How would they celebrate holidays with their families? The conversations weren't always easy—they argued and sometimes the arguments even got heated. But they kept at it because they loved each other, respected each other and they *wanted it to work*. They had a mutual goal: build a life together. They couldn't get to their goal without discussing and sifting through their biggest differences. Neither was right or wrong—they just had very different views in some pretty major areas. The only way to figure out how they'd handle life as a couple, as a team, was to talk through those different views and come to an understanding of how they wanted their life together to work. They had no choice but to hash it all out. It wasn't easy. But they did it. They came to agree on how'd they raise their kids, handle holidays with their parents, and much more.

Sure, this is a personal example, not a business one. You might be thinking, "They loved each other. I don't love the people I work with." But it shows that you can discuss even the most difficult issues if *the conversation is rooted in respect and a mutual goal*.

Constructive conflict isn't just arguing and creating friction between parties. Constructive conflict has *a purpose*. Its purpose is to identify and discuss what is really going on. It's addressing the reality of a situation, warts and all. Leaders have no choice but to deal with reality, with all its imperfections, obstacles, and disappointments. Sometimes, reality isn't very pretty, but it's *what is happening*. You can't effectively lead a team or a business if you can't deal with what's real, what's happening. In fact, when reality is ugly, when the problems you face are tough and demanding and seem insurmountable, that's when you need your diverse team the most. Your diverse team can pull together to solve even the most difficult, seemingly impossible problem, but not if they don't understand *what's really happening*. You've got to be truthful and talk about difficult subject matter head-on, including the emotions that your team members may be feeling.

A large, global, multimillion-dollar electrical distributor, serving customers all over the globe, has a woman as CEO. The electrical distribution industry is one that has long been dominated by men. That's starting to change, and more women are entering the field now, but this CEO is still one of only a handful of women CEOs in that industry. She specifically uses constructive conflict in running her company. "I use healthy argument to get to compromise and agree on a vision," she says. "A team environment with men generates great results. Many of them grew up playing sports, and they're conditioned to 'shake it off' when they disagree with someone. Coaches don't tolerate personality issues—they don't align with the goals of the team. In a team, these guys transform, adapt, and supportively mentor each other." She doesn't shy away from healthy, robust argument with her teams of men because she knows that's how they'll get to a solution. "They won't get upset. They won't pout or sulk. They'll encourage each other and support each other, just like a sports team does."

This approach to constructive conflict also calls for empathy—she believes that first and foremost, a leader's level of empathy must be high. "You've got to understand what they're feeling in order to understand how to set the vision and get buy-in from the team." She uses the example of an older man on her team who'd been in the business for ages and was resistant to a new approach the company was taking. "I could see in meetings that he wasn't on board," she stated. "His arms were crossed over his chest, his face was turning red. He looked like he was going to have a heart attack." She recognized that what the man was feeling was fear of change. Change can be scary and uncomfortable, but it's essential in business. "I realized that I needed to educate and defend our goal, but that with this individual, it was important to first get him to verbalize his reservations. I called him out by name to engage him: 'Gary, you've got more experience here than anyone. What do you see as the potential obstacles we need to address to make this successful?'" By saying this, she acknowledged his depth and breadth of experience and validated his vast knowledge. But *she also required him to help with solutions*. Her empathy made her aware of what he was feeling—fear of change, that he or his skills may not be as valued in a changing environment. Her approach reassured him, but also called on him to focus on solutions and the goal, rather than just spout negative opinions or complaints. It's a great way to guide the conversation so that it's productive, not destructive.

Here's another example of talking through differences to get to a productive resolution: Itron is a global provider of meters and technology to the utility industry. Chances are the electric, gas, or water meter on your house is made by them. Itron is headquartered in Spokane, Washington, but they also had an engineering arm in Silicon Valley. The engineers there weren't just smart brainiacs—these guys were "elite engineers"—the best of the best. True visionaries. In addition to being smart, they were also a bit arrogant. As one Itron executive put it, "They think everyone else is stupid."

Itron had huge market share, but they needed new technology to be the best in the world. Rob Neilson, former president and COO of Itron said, "We didn't want leading edge technology. We wanted *leapfrog* technology and to be out in front—way out in front of everyone else."

Itron put their brainiac engineers to work to develop the leapfrog technology they sought. At the same time, they acquired a manufacturing company in Waseca, Minnesota, that was creating innovative technology and manufacturing it, too. Rob realized it was crazy to have the Silicon Valley engineers working on tech development when the Minnesota team was already pushing ahead in that direction. His idea was to get the "best of the best" from each team together to create genius innovation. It was a no-brainer.

The dilemma? Even though everyone involved was an engineer, the two teams were actually quite "diverse." There were significant differences between the two teams: big city versus small, rural town; West Coast versus Midwest; big brain, technology design engineers versus the guys who are "primarily manufacturing support." There was also a bit of snobbery going on: the Silicon Valley guys felt disdain for the Minnesota team—they thought there was *no way* the small-town Minnesota guys could possibly have anything to contribute—they dismissed their technology as inferior simply because "the guys from the Midwest" created it. And the Minnesota team wanted to continue to do things their own way and resisted efforts to share or collaborate with the Silicon Valley guys. As Rob put it, "They never seemed to understand that they'd been acquired."

With supersized egos involved, and each team wanting to prove that they were better than, smarter than and, well, *superior* to the other, Rob had to construct a eight-step plan to bring both teams together to work productively and not start a war. Here's what he did:

Step One: He identified the key people he'd need from each team and set up a series of introductory meetings to set the goals and time-line for the development and launch of brand new technology.

Step Two: They met on neutral turf. Rob set up the first meetings in Spokane. He said, "If I'd held our first meetings in either Silicon Valley or Minnesota, they'd have been a disaster. It would have been like taking sides. These guys did not see themselves as a team—in their minds, they were competitors, even though they all worked for the same company."

Step Three: He observed in those meetings who was open-minded and viewing the situation rationally. As mentioned earlier, you can tell who's resistant to working productively: their arms are crossed defensively across their chests, or they focus on the negative. Rob observed the group dynamics and identified those who could set their egos aside and see the big picture.

Step Four: Rob also observed who the "natural influencers" were, or what I called "pilot fish" in Chapter 7. These "natural influencers" could shape the opinions and views of the team, and Rob knew he'd need them to help keep everyone on course throughout the development process.

Step Five: Rob put the open-minded engineers together with the engineers who were natural influencers/pilot fish. He knew that these two types of personalities would drive the teams. He also gave them subtle encouragement to foster communication and collaboration. For example, he'd stop by their meeting room at the end of the day to check in with them, and he'd say, "It's been a long day—why don't you guys go grab a bite and have a beer? It's on me." He knew that conversation *beyond a meeting room* would build trust because when people are sharing a meal together, they're going to talk about themselves, their families and, of course, their work. They opened up to each other and realized that "the other guy is not the enemy." As they became more open and comfortable with each other, trust was built. And through them, that trust trickled down to the rest of the team. Little by little, bit by bit, they started working collaboratively and trying ideas out on each other: "Hey, what if we did this?" They still had their big egos, but now those egos were put to work trying to be brilliant and out-think each other instead of stonewalling or dismissing each other.

Step Six: As the "superteam" began creating technology, Rob had to step in with two hard truths.

1. He told them, "You're getting there, but you're not there yet." This pushed the team to stretch and not settle for creating a good product—or even a very good one—they were pushed to create something *amazing* and revolutionary. Rob encouraged them, and made sure to acknowledge their progress and hard work, but he never let them off the hook on achieving excellence.

2. He gave them a firm—and nearly impossible—deadline. He told them, "This is what we proposed. We put it on the table and it was approved. Now we have to make it happen." Of course, the teams screamed and squawked: "We can't do that! It can't be done! It's not possible!" They begged for a longer timeline, but Rob held firm. He later said this was the exact moment when the magic happened: when the team realized that they had no choice but to meet the deadline, they also realized *the only way they could do it was to rely on each other.*

Step Seven: Let them figure it out. Rob told me this is where a leader must have a strong stomach. "They freaked out. They groused and grumbled. They argued. But then they got down to business and got to work." He advises that this stage is where leaders need to stand firm and not cave in to complaints or panic. Good teams are capable of greatness, but they won't discover that greatness unless they are pushed to tap into their brilliance. Rob also cautioned that, at this stage, expect others to ask to pull team members apart. For example, the sales or marketing department may say they need to have time with a team member or two to complete their work, but Rob believes it's crucial to say no to those requests. "Once that team is on the edge of breakthrough, you've got to keep them together, keep them working on their goal or nothing will ever get done."

Step Eight: Track progress. Establish checkpoints where the whole group gathers to discuss the project. This gives them not only a chance to vent to their colleagues, it gives them *visibility*. In Rob's case, he said, "These guys were proud! They'd just done the impossible! They wanted to show off what they'd done. Let them brag. Let them have meetings where 'updates' turn into accomplishment sharing. They've earned it."

Itron's core team of 25 delivered on the impossible. They brought leapfrog revolutionary technology to market in record time. It was a defining moment for the company and for Rob as a leader.

Most leaders like to have control and make decisions—that's one of the characteristics that make them effective at being in charge. But Rob said his process taught him to let go and that doing so was what enabled the breakthrough, brilliant technology that Itron brought to market. He said, "What would have killed this would have been dictating the process. If Itron had dictated how the engineering teams were to work together, it never would have worked. They had to have ownership. It had to come from them. Once it did, they were unstoppable."

Rob's eight-step plan can work for any team. Aside from the steps, I like the insights he shared about what a leader should expect at various stages of the process. A key subject that leaders need to be prepared to address is what to do about naysayers and derailers.

DEALING WITH NAYSAYERS AND DERAILERS

It's inevitable: no matter how good of a leader you are, you'll encounter those people on your team who are naysayers. They're negative, they don't believe anything is worth trying, they say nothing will work, and they'll give you a thousand reasons why everything is a bad idea. And there are "derailers"— people who may not outwardly appear to be negative, but they find subtle ways to derail or sabotage efforts along the way. Perhaps they withhold key information from a team member, or they ignore a deadline, or they cast doubt about a project or a person. For whatever reason, they're not on board, and they try to derail the best efforts of the rest of the team. Either kind of person can suck the lifeblood and enthusiasm out of your team, so you've got to have a plan for dealing with them when they pop up.

Speaking of popping up, dealing with naysayers is a little like playing "Whack-a-Mole," the arcade game. If you haven't played "Whack-a-Mole," it works like this: the player has a rubber mallet and has to whack down "moles" that pop up out of the game board. The moles are everywhere—just when you get one whacked down, another pops up. It never ends. So it is with naysayers and negative people. There are several approaches that are effective in controlling naysayers and derailers so they don't end up controlling your team:

- *Use positive reinforcement.* Meet their negatives head-on with positives. When they say, "I doubt we can complete this by next Friday" you say, "I know it will be a challenge, but I am confident you can do it." Or when the naysayer says, "I don't think our sales team is prepared to go down this road," you say, "I understand you have doubts. Let's talk about what can be done to ensure success." Essentially, don't let the naysayer lead you down a path of why things won't work. It's a path with no end. Don't take the bait. Turn the conversation to the positive and keep doing that. The naysayer will eventually exhaust themselves trying to get you to keep them company on their negative journey.

- *Allay their fears.* Earlier in this chapter, I mentioned the electrical distributor CEO's comment about fear of change being at the root of resistance. She's absolutely right. Fear is, by nature, a negative force. It's a negative emotion and it yields negative results. But *fear is real*, so you can't simply dismiss an associate's fear. Identify what they are concerned about and work to allay their fears. For example, when a naysayer expresses a negative view of a project say, "I know this is a difficult project and I know you're anxious about the outcome. But we have confidence in you and the team. Your skills are what we need for this. What can I do to support you?" When someone is afraid, they can't be optimistic or enthusiastic or supportive. Allay their fears and you'll see a different side of them, a better side.

- *Let the team become their own police force.* Teams have a certain chemistry. When everyone is moving forward and working together, there's not much room for naysayers or derailers. Good teams don't tolerate them long. As a leader, your instinct may be to step in when you see or hear negative behavior, but often the best remedy is to let the team work it out themselves. Peer pressure is powerful. The team will find ways—overt or not—to put the naysayer or derailer in their place. We all like acceptance. It's human nature to want to be liked and accepted, especially by our peers. So when peers chastise or scold an individual on a team, it's embarrassing for that team member. Their bad behavior usually stops pretty quickly. Let your team establish and enforce their own rules of acceptable behavior.

- *Change the People.* One of my clients had a mantra for working with difficult, negative people. They said, "You can change the people. Or you can: Change. The. People." What they meant by that was, when working with a negative person, do all that you can to *transform them and help them better themselves.* Point out how their behavior affects others. Explain that it's not acceptable. Give them a chance to fix themselves.

But if you've tried that and the negative behavior persists, then make a change. Get rid of that person. Move them off the team. It sounds harsh, but it's not, because you'll give the negative person every chance to change. If they won't, then you'll need to "change the person." Let them go.

This approach is highly effective when you tell the negative individual that there are only two options: Change the person. Or: Change. The. Person. *It's up to them.* If they do *their* part, you'll never have to "change the person."

CHAPTER 9 ➤➤
Don't Just Hire People Who Are Like You—But *Avoid Tokenism*

Years ago, I worked for a major ad agency and our biggest client was a car company. The auto industry has become more diverse, but it's still pretty much dominated by White male executives. At the time that I worked with this car company, there were some women in top positions, but no people of color in executive positions. In fact, there were very few people of color in the organization at all.

This car company had a big heart, a corporate soul, if you will. They always tried to do the right thing, not just the most cost-efficient thing. They rarely terminated anyone—they'd demote them to some lower level job if the individual wasn't performing. Their corporate culture was big on caring for their employees.

As "diversity" became a topic that more and more large companies were facing and addressing, this car company tried to address it too. They promoted Barbara, an administrative assistant, to the role of diversity marketing manager. Barbara is Black. She fit their requirements for "diversity" because of her race. The problem was, she didn't fit the requirements for a *marketing professional*, nor had she ever *managed* anyone or any department or project before. She's been in a *support* role her entire career. She was outstanding in that role, and—you guessed it—she was terrible in the role of diversity marketing manager.

The car company did what they thought was right. They wanted to show their associates and the world that they embraced diversity and promoted from within. Heck, they wanted to show that they even had a diversity marketing department—with its own manager! But it was a house of cards and was doomed to fail from the start. There was no diversity work being done and, therefore, the "diversity marketing manager" had no one and nothing to "manage." More important, she didn't know the first thing about marketing. She had no training, background, or experience in marketing of any kind.

Barbara tried mightily to learn her job and make contributions. But she was ineffective because she was in over her head. She knew nothing about marketing—not even the "lingo"—how could she? She'd never even been in marketing meetings before!

Because Barbara didn't have the skills to do her job, it was a disaster. She made bad decisions and costly mistakes because she lacked experience. It was very difficult for all the people who worked with her because they had to stop and explain the most basic things to her. They had to spend tons of time discussing fundamentals, essentially training her, on a daily basis. This made her coworkers frustrated, and sometimes even mad. They were exasperated, impatient, and resentful. Worst of all, they didn't respect her in her position because she clearly wasn't qualified. Behind her back, there was eye-rolling and conversations about how "she only got the job because she's Black."

Poor Barbara. None of it was her fault. She didn't hire on at the company as a marketing manager, she didn't aspire to that role, heck, she didn't even apply for the job! Upper management just appointed her to it because of the color of her skin.

It was a terrible decision. There was no way she could succeed—she didn't have the training, background, or resources. She had nothing but a title and everyone knew it. And this terrible decision caused a domino effect that put their entire diversity initiative in a bad light:

1. Promote Barbara because she's Black.
2. Barbara doesn't have the skills to do the job.
3. Barbara fails in the role because she's not qualified.
4. Everyone sees Barbara failing and they say, "She can't do the job. She only got it because she's Black."
5. Because she's not qualified or effective, everyone dismisses Barbara.
6. And they also *dismiss the entire diversity effort because it can't be taken seriously.* Ugh—what a mess!

Barbara ultimately left the company. I think her experience in that role was so painful that she no longer wanted to work there. She knew people resented her and didn't respect her in the position. There were whispers of "tokenism." She could feel the eye-rolling and she was miserable.

This is not what the car company intended. They meant well. They truly wanted to do the right thing, but it was a colossal mistake. They inadvertently damaged Barbara's reputation within the company, which damaged their entire diversity effort—along with management's credibility with decision making. And, at the end, they lost a good employee. What an awful outcome all the way around!

In hindsight, it seems so obvious: any time you put someone in a position they're not qualified for or ready for, and you give them zero training and support, they're almost certainly going to fail. No matter how much you like a person or how sincerely you believe in equality and giving people chances, if that individual is not qualified to do a job, but they get the job because they have a certain skin color, or a disability or they are a certain gender or belong to any other minority group, you've probably made a bad decision.

But you're reading this book because you value diversity. You know it's important, and you want diverse perspectives and experience on your team. What should you do when it comes to hiring? How do you get the talent you need and avoid creating a situation like the one Barbara was in?

IT'S NOT AS SIMPLE AS "THE BEST PERSON FOR THE JOB"

You've heard it: "*Just hire the best person for the job.*" That's a good goal, but in today's business world that approach doesn't always go far enough. The truth is—and business psychology supports this— we all gravitate to people who are like us. We gravitate to those who either look like us, have similar backgrounds or experience, or share our views. It's doesn't make us bad people—it's how we are wired as humans. We seek out—and are most comfortable with— those who are similar to us.

But we need diversity to be leading edge and innovative. How do you hire diverse talent and avoid tokenism?

BRING IT BACK TO BUSINESS

I think some business hires are made so that the company, or the hiring executive, can "check the diversity box" and feel they've done the right thing when it comes to bringing diverse talent on board. But as the case with Barbara showed, if you don't take care of the business, you're not moving forward; you're just creating problems of a different nature.

When I say "taking care of the business," I mean using business goals and business objectives as your driving motivation for diverse hires, not some politically or socially correct mindset or "we are the world" mentality. I'm not putting those motivations down—but *you're running a business*, not a campfire "kumbaya" singalong.

Start with the business situation that is calling for diverse talent. For example, when CoverGirl cosmetics launched ads with their first Muslim model wearing a hijab, it wasn't to appease liberal customers or demonstrate how trendy and inclusive they are. The Muslim personal cosmetics and personal care market is worth more than $54 billion as of this writing and is expected to exceed more than *$80 billion* in the next few years. There are millions of Muslim women who want to express their faith *and* that they're fashion forward, and makeup lets them do that. Sure, CoverGirl does get credit for being inclusive with this ad campaign, but there is a true *business opportunity* at the root of it, and that's true of all successful business initiatives.

DON'T HIRE THE WRONG PERSON—JUST TO SATISFY A DESIRE FOR DIVERSITY

The tech industry is closely watched for so many reasons: business growth, jobs creation, innovative products, and global impact as the whole world will eventually be online and connected to one another. Diversity hasn't been tech's strength though—most tech firms are still overwhelmingly staffed by White men. Tech firms are trying to change this and that's a good thing. But at a Denver tech conference, a panelist stated that the next hire at her company would be a person of color. A fellow panelist quickly chimed in and urged caution: "Be careful about making that next person a token and making them representative of everyone else that is not like your current team." It was wise advice.

It's good to look for opportunities to diversify your team, but I like how Julie Penner of TechStars sees diverse hiring: she sees it as "what's next?" That's a great way to keep diversity rooted in business and avoid tokenism. When CoverGirl looked for markets that are expanding, they saw the growth of the Muslim market and their research found that observant Muslim women want to adhere to their faith and still look pretty. Expanding their marketing efforts to reach Muslim women was a logical "what's next?" step.

TOP DOWN BEATS BOTTOM UP

Adding diverse people at the *beginning* of the hiring process, or top of the hiring funnel, is the way to start. That way, you're looking at a candidate pool that is diverse and then making the best decision for your company from the pool of candidates. That certainly beats hiring a diverse person and hoping you end up with the right skill set and chemistry for your team. If you include diverse talent *throughout* the process, you'll find that your hires will become more diverse over time *and* you'll be hiring the right person for the job.

How do you find good candidates to include at the beginning of the hiring process?

Here are four effective strategies that companies use:

1. Recruit in nontraditional venues.
   - If you always advertise job openings in the same forums or recruit from the same schools or peer groups, you'll continue to attract the same kind of talent you've always gotten. Think of new, nontraditional ways or venues to broaden your recruiting. The *New York Times* works with the National Association of Black Journalists to broaden their applicant pool. They've also developed outreach programs in historically Black colleges and universities to attract top Black talent.
2. Provide mentoring.
   - Make sure that your diverse associates have the mentoring they need to succeed. Mentoring not only guides associates in decision making and problem solving, it also gives the person being mentored a sounding board to discuss corporate culture and what it takes to be successful in a particular environment or team.

3. Offer parental leave or leaves of absence and review your jobs for pay equity.
   - Research shows that, even in married households with two working spouses, women shoulder more of the household work and responsibilities than men do. And many women are single parents, caring for aging parents or loved ones in addition to juggling a busy household and a full-time job. If you want to attract more women associates to your company or team, it helps if you have benefits in place that women tend to need. The ability to take time off to care for a family member speaks volumes about a company and may help you recruit women executives who are in demand. The same goes for pay equity. If you want top talent, compensate fairly and equitably.
4. Standardize the hiring questions you use.
   - This is a subtle but important step. Because we tend to gravitate to people who are like we are, we tend to speak in certain ways when we are around those who are like us. You don't want to "tilt" a candidate's response to an interview question, so it's important to ask questions in the same way. This helps avoid any bias in interviewing and gives candidates the same opportunity in responding to questions.

When you hire talented associates who are not like you, and you do it the right way, for the right reasons, you'll be amazed at how your team will perform. You'll not only avoid tokenism, you'll reach new levels of productivity, employee engagement, and financial success. Your business will flourish and so will your team.

In the next chapter, we'll tackle the next level in managing diverse teams: how to navigate the waters of promotions and professional development for your people.

CHAPTER 10

Navigating the Waters of Promotions and Professional Development

Okay, so you've built a diverse team. You're proud of your hiring efforts and you've seen firsthand how well a diverse team can perform: they're solving problems and thinking in broader and more creative ways. They—and your business—are flourishing.

You want to reward your top performers with promotions and professional advancement. You want to see your diverse talent rise through the organization. But you don't want to find yourself in a situation like the one I described in the last chapter with Barbara. You know it's crucial to promote the right people for the right reasons.

Here's a rather weird fact: *only two in five American workers believe merit counts for most job advancement.* The other factors that are named as affecting promotions at work are: connections, seniority, and luck. Each one of those can be viewed as pretty depressing and demoralizing. Let's look at why:

- Connections. What if you don't have any? What if the circle of people in your social or professional network aren't that influential? Or they're not that well connected themselves? Or wealthy? A company in Texas that owns assisted living communities for the elderly had tremendous difficulty adding people of color to their board of directors. They valued diversity and tried mightily to find diverse talent for their board, but without much success. Why? Because one of the criteria for being on their board was the board member's ability to help them fundraise. To be effective at fundraising, *really* effective (for example, raising hundreds of thousands or millions of dollars), you've got to know wealthy people and lots of them. And you've got to know them well enough to be able to *call them and ask for money.* Many minority professionals simply don't have the breadth of connections of people at that income/economic level. So, without intending it, the field of potential board members for this company disproportionately skewed to White candidates because of their connections.

- Seniority. This one really stinks. Most of us have, at one time or another, worked with someone who was average at best, but had been with the organization forever. Just because you've put in time at a company doesn't necessarily equate to talent—it doesn't mean you're the best in your field or department. In fact, for many people, the longer they stay with a company or organization, the more they start to "coast"—just doing what they need to do to sail along. They're not that ambitious and they don't put forth that much effort, but they know the corporate culture well enough to know what to do to get by. Another reason that promoting someone strictly based on their seniority stinks: *simply working for an organization for a long time does not make someone a leader*. Leaders have specific skills and characteristics. Leading others is tough. Just because someone has clocked time with an organization does not mean they can lead.

- Luck. This is the most ambiguous reason for why someone thinks another person got promoted. "Luck" implies unfairness—that someone "lucked into" a position while another, more worthy, employee was passed over. Luck is an emotionally loaded word. I think many people who say a coworker got promoted because they were "lucky" are bitter or resentful about that person's promotion. It's hard to know for certain. But the perception of luck when it comes to professional advancement is certainly not a good perception.

Let's talk about perception. If only two in five Americans believe that merit accounts for job advancement, then the majority of workers perceive that these *other* reasons are why people get promoted. Rightly or wrongly, accurately or inaccurately, that's their *perception*. It means that good workers don't believe that their efforts will necessarily result in their advancement. They're skeptical—and perhaps even a little bitter.

Here are two more factors to add to the list of perceptions: tokenism and favoritism. In the last chapter, we talked about the danger of tokenism and the negative effect it can have on an entire team or organization. Favoritism can be just as negative and destructive. When someone gets promoted because they are favored—or they are *perceived to be favored* (perhaps they are buddies with the boss or share similar hobbies or interests with those who are higher up or perhaps they are just adept at brown-nosing)—that individual will never get the respect of others. It's viewed as "unearned."

Whether these types of negative perceptions are true or not is immaterial. *If people think you promoted someone based on any factor other than merit, your credibility as a leader is just as damaged as the person you promoted.*

So how do you change this dynamic? How can you overcome the distrust people feel when it comes to why you promoted someone? First, you have to understand why the distrust exists in the first place.

Distrust begins when it's not clear to employees what the rules of the game are for advancement. When workers can't understand why or how some people are getting promoted and others aren't, they feel distrust. This is especially true if qualified people are being passed over for those who are less qualified. *If it's not clear why someone received a promotion, then employees end up filling in the explanation for themselves* and it's usually a negative perception, like bias or seniority. You don't want that—you want the only perception for a promotion to be one of merit.

Here are three ways to ensure that your team knows that you utilize fair corporate promotion practices:

1. Clarify the criteria used for promotion consideration. *Make it concrete and specific.* Use objective metrics for performance, such as increased sales, profitability, reduced employee turnover, or new product development. If the criteria for advancement is spelled out clearly, it's not subjective. It's fair. This helps refute any note of favoritism, seniority, luck, or bias.
2. Establish clear standards and expectations for *all* employees.
3. Give clear feedback on employee performance and coach employees on improving their deficiencies. Train your managers to do the same.

This last point is crucial: you must help your people see where they are deficient—they need to know what's holding them back professionally. And then help them overcome those deficiencies to achieve their potential.

As a leader, you're responsible for professionally developing your people. You want them to be well-positioned for promotion, but you must prepare them. In many companies or organizations, job competency alone will not be enough to earn a promotion. Soft skills are highly valued and many employees don't have them at all or don't focus enough on honing them. Soft skills include relationship skills, such as communicating effectively with others, resolving conflict, negotiating, demonstrating teamwork, and developing networks within the organization. When someone is promoted, they become a role model to others in the organization. Top executives want to have confidence that that person will *behave* a certain way.

David worked for a large, Fortune 500 company. He was very good at his job, which involved lots of reports and number crunching. Anything you wanted to know about sales, revenue, or year-over-year performance, David could tell you instantly. He was adept at analysis, and he worked hard putting in long hours. He was absolutely dedicated to the company. Although he'd made it to the level of director, he was never going to become a vice president. He kept getting passed over for promotion and he didn't know why. But everyone else did.

David loved to argue. He loved to debate people and "prove them wrong." He had a strong need to be right, and because he'd been with the company a long time, he felt he was the authority on everything. He would pick little fights or quarrels with coworkers just so he could demonstrate that he was correct. He felt most other people weren't as smart as he was and his disdain was apparent to others. In meetings, he used his numbers and reports as a shield—he couldn't just *discuss* an issue. He was combative. He was very smart and very, very good at his job, but he had zero people skills. No one wanted to work with him, even as a peer, so why would management want to promote him to a leadership position? Even though David was terrific at the core competency part of his job, he had no soft skills. Therefore, he was never promoted beyond the director level. Over time, he became very bitter about being passed over and he greatly resented those who did get promoted. He'd make snide comments in meetings and try to undermine them behind their backs. It was a bad situation that only got worse as time went on.

Maybe if he'd had some clear and honest feedback along the way, he could have worked on his relationship skills. Or if the company had spelled out the specific skills they look for in leaders and helped him by coaching him on his communication skills, training him and developing him, he might have been able to grow in that area. We'll never know. But it's a shame, because David had great skills—he just wasn't well-rounded, particularly in the soft skills and communications area.

Being direct in talking with people about their deficiencies is uncomfortable. I think that's why David's managers didn't address his behavior with him. It was easier to just let it go. But it's not fair to the employee. They can't address what they aren't aware of. As a leader, it's your job to help your associates identify the areas that they need to work on and also provide resources to assist them. Yes, the employee has to do the hard work of polishing their skills, but you must provide the awareness of what's needed and point them to the path that will help them grow.

Laura was an employee at my company for several years. She was Hispanic and foreign born and English was her second language. Laura had worked very, very hard to become fluent in English and her language skills were impressive. However, her written skills did not match her verbal fluency. She lacked the ability to write a professional, well-worded memo or a proposal in English. She was smart and hard-working and wanted to move up within the company.

We discussed what was holding her back from being promoted to the next level. I told her very clearly that it wasn't the quality of her work or her dedication, it was her written communication skills. I told her that the position she wanted required significant writing skills, from memos to formal presentations, and that her writing was not up to that standard. She understood and was eager to improve.

We found a class that was geared specifically to improving written business communication. It was a night class on Tuesdays and Thursdays from 5 p.m. to 8 p.m. I told Laura that not only would I pay for the class, I would make sure she was able to leave the office on those days at 4 p.m. so that she could make it to the class on time.

Laura jumped at the chance to take the class and her commitment impressed me. Taking a three-hour night class, twice a week, when you've already put in a full day at the office is a *lot* of commitment. And the course was three months long. This was a great solution for our mutual goal, "preparing Laura for advancement," but it was far harder on Laura than it was on me, the company owner. All I had to do was cover the expense and make sure she could leave the office early two days a week. She was the one who put in the real effort: the classes, the homework, the commitment to long days.

But it worked. Laura tackled the class and excelled. She polished and perfected her writing skills and eventually was promoted, on *merit*. No one could say she didn't earn it. She not only earned the promotion, she also earned the respect of all of her coworkers because they knew she was taking a class and they saw how hard she worked for what she wanted.

It's up to your employees to put in the work to earn a promotion. But *it's up to you to make the playing field a level one.* You must provide your team members with the tools and the means to acquire or hone the skills they need. In Laura's case, I had to provide money and time off. But she's the one who had to follow through, for months, committing hours and hours of her personal time to bettering her skills. When she wasn't ready for the promotion, she understood why. And when she tackled her deficiency of weak writing skills, she was ready to succeed—and it was clear to everyone why she was promoted: *she was qualified and had earned it.*

Here are six steps for professional development that are fair and will yield the best outcome in preparing your diverse team for advancement:

1. Identify the areas of deficiency or focus for your associates. Be clear about what specific skills they need that will position them for advancement.

2. If you have an HR department, work with them to identify and provide the appropriate resources to educate and develop your team.

3. If you don't have an HR department, meet with your team members individually to map out their growth plans and what they'll need to succeed and achieve that growth.

4. Discuss what the company or organization can provide to assist them in their growth journey.

5. Be clear that this is a team effort: they must be just as committed to their growth and development as you are. This may require them to invest significant time and effort to build their skill set.

6. Set up ongoing meetings to review their progress and provide coaching and feedback.

These steps provide a blueprint for navigating the waters of advancement. You want your team to reach their full potential and succeed, but you need to ensure that everyone understands exactly what is expected to earn a promotion. The criteria should be objective and measurable—and fair. If you have employees who are deficient in specific areas and these deficiencies are holding them back, tell them! Show them how they can progress and what the company can do to assist them in achieving their goals. You can groom them and prepare them for advancement, but they have to do the work. The result will be not only employees who have "skin in the game" and are proud of their accomplishments and achievements but also an organizational reputation for employee advancement—and fairness.

When you hire talented associates who are not like you, and you do it the right way, for the right reasons, you'll be amazed at how your team will perform. You'll not only avoid tokenism, you'll reach new levels of productivity, employee engagement, and financial success. Your business will flourish and so will your team.

In the next chapter, we'll tackle the next level in managing diverse teams: how and when to make accommodations for your employees.

CHAPTER 11 ➡

Making Accommodations for Employees—Do You Have To?

Sally Shoquist was the executive vice president of media strategy at a large global ad agency. She oversaw a department of 60 associates, 90 percent of whom were women. Of the 90 percent who were women, about half were moms with young children. Sally joked, "And I think the rest were pregnant! There was *always* someone either leaving for maternity leave or returning from maternity leave. We had to juggle workloads *constantly*." There are certain industries that tend to have lots of female workers: healthcare, teaching, human resources—and media. It wasn't unusual for Sally to have an almost all-women department. What she had to learn to manage were the near constant requests from her team for time off, permission to leave the office early to pick up a kid, have a meeting with a teacher, stay home with a sick child. These working moms had a lot to juggle, like most moms do.

At the time, working from home wasn't nearly as common as it is now. Furthermore, ad agencies are in the client service business—they must be responsive to their client needs, no matter how inconvenient those needs may be. Sally's challenge was to try to balance the requests of her employees for being *out of the office* with running a department that had lots of meetings with clients *in the office*. In addition to face-to-face meetings with clients, there were endless internal meetings as well. To have people constantly absent from these important meetings was problematic. And to complicate matters even more, there were several associates who weren't moms. They felt resentment that the moms received "special treatment" and got to leave early or work from home. Sally had to figure out a way to accommodate her employees without alienating others and without the work suffering.

At first, she tried to be flexible with requests for time off or to leave the office early for family situations, but it always seemed to backfire. Deadlines were missed. The single women, most of whom had no children, resented what they saw as the "privilege" of those with families coming and going as they pleased. Complaints such as, "Why should

I have to work an eight- or nine-hour day just because I don't have kids and my counterpart with a kid gets to sail out of here at 2:30? Or not come into the office until 11 a.m.? It's not fair!" were common. Frustrations mounted with *everyone*, because scheduling a simple meeting became a monumental task of coordination. When things didn't go smoothly, there was finger-pointing and blame. Sally's once cohesive team was on the verge of collapsing into "us versus them," moms versus non-moms factions. She wracked her brain trying to think of innovative, clever ways to accommodate everyone that were fair to all. But she just couldn't figure out a system that would work for all her team members and still achieve the quality work they were known for.

Then she had an epiphany: she didn't have to have the answer! Why was it up to *her* to solve this problem? She had smart people in her department: why not task *them* with coming up with a way to achieve *their* desired outcome? She sat them all down, held a meeting, and told them that she was supportive of their busy, demanding lives and she understood that often those personal demands conflicted with time in the office. She stated that she wanted to be able to accommodate people, but *she also had a business to run.* They wouldn't have jobs if it weren't for their clients, so the work had to be a priority. She gave them a challenge: work together to figure out a system where people get the flexibility that they need, but the company gets the quality, on-time work that it needs. She told them it was up to *them* to determine what was reasonable and fair and how to make sure the work kept moving forward. Then she left them alone to hash it out.

In Chapter 8, this same approach was used by Itron when it came to creating a new product technology. The approach works because when people are given the opportunity to *resolve their own issues with their colleagues, they tend to come up with viable, workable solutions that are also fair to the team members.* And, usually, what they come up with is something a manager or department head would never have dreamed up. They're highly motivated to find answers and, because *they* develop the solution, there's little to no bickering within the team. In Sally's case, her team came up with a fairly complex, but very fair, system of rotating people in and out of the office. They made sure the work was covered and created backup plans for when more people needed to be out and to cover emergencies. They even made back-up plans for the backup plans! The system they created accommodated their schedules, ensured the work would be up to par, and struck a balance for all involved, whether they were moms or not.

When Sally's team presented her with the plan and system they'd come up with, she approved it—with a caveat: she made it crystal clear that the expectation was that the work could not suffer. She was willing to try something new, but if the quality of the work went down, if team communication suffered or if there were bickering and squabbling among them, she let them know that would be the end of their new flex program.

Not one of her team members disappointed. In fact, they excelled and put even *more* into their work than before. They performed at a higher level and were more enthusiastic about work than ever. They enjoyed their newfound freedom and flexibility and there was no way they were going to jeopardize it, so they worked more productively and better than they ever had.

Sally accommodated her team. She didn't have to, but by doing so, employee engagement and loyalty spiked up and the sense of "teamness" was stronger than ever. The question is, do you have to accommodate your employees or team members? And if so, how far do you have to go?

TELECOMMUTING, PARENTHOOD, AND PRAYERS, OH MY!

In the United States, the law is very clear regarding employers accommodating employees, but the law specifically protects those with disabilities. The Americans with Disabilities Act (ADA) states that employers must make reasonable accommodations to enable an employee to do his or her job despite having a disability. But in Sally's case, her team didn't have disabilities—they just had requests. She didn't *have to* accommodate them.

As a leader, you face all kinds of requests from your team. Some may be reasonable, some unreasonable. Some may require legal compliance. If you're in doubt about what may be required of you or your company, check with your HR department or an employment attorney.

But when it comes to accommodating associates who are not like you, and they want things you're not accustomed to providing, do you have to?

A Harley-Davidson dealer I know has an employee who is Muslim. Muslims are expected to pray five times a day: at predawn, noon, afternoon, sunset, and night. Praying doesn't take that long—most Muslims say their prayers can be completed in about five minutes, but preprayer ritual washing can take just as long or even a few minutes longer. The times that prayers are most likely to conflict with work schedules are the daytime prayers: noon, afternoon, and sunset. This can put both the employee and employer or leader in a tough spot. Most employers want to accommodate their employees' faith requirements, but at the same time they have a business to run. In the case of the Harley-Davidson dealer, this particular employee, Hossam, was a technician, a mechanic who worked on the motorcycles that were brought into the dealership for repair. Mechanics' time at most dealerships is billed at an hourly rate to the customer, so keeping track of the exact number of hours worked is critical to how the department runs and the revenue it generates. Additionally, the work must get done in a certain shift each day. It's not okay to take longer with repairs when a customer is expecting to have their bike back on a given day. The dealer wanted to accommodate Hossam, but had to find a way to still get the repair work done, despite three interruptions per shift.

Together, the dealer and Hossam discussed how this could work. Most dealerships keep their showrooms open until 7 p.m. or later to meet with customers who are thinking of purchasing a bike, but their service departments and body shops usually close earlier, at 5 p.m. or 6 p.m. The dealer and Hossam agreed that Hossam would come earlier to work or stay later to finish customer repairs. Let's say that the preprayer ritual and the time to pray three times each day added up to a total of 40 minutes. Hossam's shift was expanded to add in the extra 40 minutes. He usually stayed the extra time in the evenings, when the dealership was still open but the service department was closed. This solution worked because he was able to observe his faith rituals, put in the required number of work hours, and get the repair work done on time to satisfy customers.

There are two more aspects of this story that must be mentioned. The first was that none of the dealer's other employees were Muslim. They didn't understand the requirements of Islamic faith. Someone praying five times a day was completely new to them, even a bit "odd." And several employees voiced their resentment that Hossam got multiple breaks throughout the day, but they didn't. The Harley dealer handled this beautifully: he had a meeting with the entire staff and explained the basic tenets of Islam and that observant Muslims pray five times a day. He said he understood that *the way they saw it* one employee was getting more time off than the rest, but that these were not breaks—they were just an aspect of faith of an observant Muslim associate. He explained what he and Hossam had worked out and said, "So don't be surprised when you see Hossam staying later than the rest of the guys in the service department. He's making sure his work gets finished on time and the customers' motorcycles are repaired when we promised they would be." No one could argue with this. It was *fair*. The team was educated and informed about a religion they were unfamiliar with, their concerns about fairness were addressed, and the work got done as promised to customers. Being proactive about talking to his associates was key—the dealer didn't wait until resentment had festered and problems arose. He made it a priority to figure out a solution with his Muslim mechanic right away and then informed the rest of the staff how they'd be accommodating this employee going forward.

The second issue the dealer had to contend with was *where* his Muslim employee could pray. Again, the dealer and Hossam talked through the issue and decided that the conference room would be the best option. However, the dealer cautioned that, because he *has a business to run,* the conference room might not always be available. In other words, he offered the conference room as an option and it was to be Hossam's first place to go to pray, but if there was a meeting or training taking place, he would need to find another place. Hossam wasn't *entitled* to use the conference room; it was offered as the first place to explore. If the conference room was occupied, Hossam would ask to use a fellow employee's office. If that wasn't possible, Hossam would then have to find a place to pray on his own. He understood this and a couple of times he has had to pray in his car, which isn't ideal, but works in a pinch.

There are several things that this Harley dealer did right:

- He *recognized that he had someone on his team who was "not like him"* (or anyone else, for that matter) and accepted right away that the employee needed to stop work to pray several times per day.
- He and his employee talked together and came to *mutual agreement* on how they would structure his work to accommodate the prayers *and* the dealership's need to keep the work moving along on time.
- He *held a meeting* with all associates to explain why Hossam's work schedule varied from the rest and what they should expect to see: he'd be working a bit longer each night. This meeting also served to *educate the team about observing a faith they knew nothing about and gave them a chance to ask questions.* It squashed resentment, rumor, and speculation—when everyone is in the loop and understands what is going on and why, and when the solutions offered are *fair and respectful to all*, people get on board. Usually what drives employees nuts is when they don't understand something or they don't think something is fair. Informing them and discussing fair solutions are powerful tools to eliminating resentment and fostering understanding.
- He *did his best to accommodate* Hossam regarding a place to pray, offering two options, but made it clear that, ultimately, Hossam would have to figure out the *where*. The dealer wasn't going to build him a prayer room. And Hossam didn't expect that—he just wanted to be able to observe his faith.

A really interesting thing happened with the *other* employees at the dealership: many times, customers would come in and see Hossam's turban and comment to another employee, "I didn't know you had a Muslim employee." And the other employee would respond with something like, "Yes! He's been with us for two years and it's interesting, because he needs to pray five times a day, even at work, and he does. He goes in our conference room and prays and he keeps a prayer mat here at the dealership in his locker. This dealership is really supportive of diversity." The other employees were proud! They were subtly *bragging* about their Muslim coworker—*and the dealership*. They viewed all of it as progressive and inclusive, and they were proud to be a part of it and eager to talk about it. Even though they weren't Muslim, they became ambassadors for Hossam and inclusion without even realizing it.

BRING IT BACK TO BUSINESS

In the examples above, both Sally and the Harley dealer made it work with their teams by bringing it back to business. The issue wasn't about wanting to or not wanting to accommodate an employee: it was "how can I do so and still accomplish what we need to as a business?" They were able to sincerely state that they'd be happy to accommodate an employee's needs, *but they also had a business to run*. In other words, the employee's needs or wishes couldn't override the *business of running the business*.

Here's another example of a leader who accommodated an employee "not like them"—this time, the accommodation was regarding cultural norms. The general manager of a five-star luxury hotel told me about a woman they hired at the front desk of their San Francisco property to check guests in and out. The woman is Japanese and speaks both English and Japanese fluently, so her language skills are valuable in this diverse and international city.

But language isn't the only way to communicate with customers— eye contact and gestures and demeanor are also powerful communication tools. In the United States and much of Europe, making direct eye contact is considered respectful. It communicates that you are giving the other person your full attention. But in some cultures, direct eye contact is considered rude. It can be viewed as confrontational, disrespectful, arrogant, or even flirtatious.

The luxury resort's "corporate culture" was to greet every customer and use direct eye contact with the customer *at all times*. This was part of their employee training and it was expected, especially of those in prominent, high visibility positions, such as the front desk of the hotel. But making direct eye contact for the Japanese woman was extremely uncomfortable. Nothing in her background or culture made it acceptable, no matter how common it is in Western society.

Her discomfort with eye contact became evident to her manager and the manager spoke with her about it and asked why she wouldn't look customers in the eye. Her manager interpreted it as lack of confidence or shyness, but that wasn't the case. The Japanese woman told her that, try as she might, she simply couldn't break the habit of looking down or looking away when talking to customers.

The hotel's objective was to make every customer feel acknowledged, special, and valued. They did this by providing exceptional customer service and part of that is eye contact. But the manager realized that eye contact *wasn't the only way* to acknowledge customers and make them feel valued and special. The manager and her Japanese associate discussed other ways to accomplish the goal and came up with a method that worked for them: the Japanese front desk associate would use every customer's title and last name (for example, "Thank you, Mr. Peterson") in virtually every sentence, while nodding affirmatively to convey that requests were understood and that the customer's needs would be taken care of. So if a guest asked for a late checkout or a newspaper to be delivered to their room, the Japanese associate would reply, "Yes, of course, Ms. Carron, we will deliver the *New York Times* to your room in the next 20 minutes. Is there anything else we can provide for you, Ms. Carron?" This approached worked because:

- The repeated use of the guest's title and name conveyed *attention and respect*.
- Reiterating the request conveyed *understanding and action*.
- Nodding the head conveyed that the request was *no trouble* at all.

As a leader, you may not always be able to accommodate employee requests. But when you can, you should. Why not? Flexibility costs little or nothing, but can yield tremendous employee engagement and loyalty. And *you don't have to figure it all out by yourself.* Enlist the help of your team members. Work with them to identify ways that you can meet their requests and still accomplish your business goals. What you mutually come up with may surprise you—solutions and ideas may be more creative, flexible, and innovative than you ever imagined.

You have a business to run. But your business will run even better when you accommodate employees who may be "not like you."

Conclusion

You know that a diverse workforce leads to better decisions and solutions—it has been proven to grow business and profits.

But when the person in the next cube or office is different from you, friction can arise. It's not easy working with people who are not like you. And if you're the leader of a diverse team, the challenges are unquestionably multiplied.

But it's worth it. And *you know this* because you picked up this book and invested the time to read it. Diversity isn't going away. It's not a fad. You will continue to work alongside people who are not like you for the rest of your career. In fact, the workplace will become even more diverse in the future as technology brings more and more people together across the globe and across every industry.

When others are struggling to understand different coworkers, different viewpoints, and different cultural norms and backgrounds, you'll know what to do. You'll be ahead of so many others. You're already ahead. You can follow the steps to "meet and greet" and how to break the ice. You'll know to look for and find common ground.

You'll know what to say, and what *not* to. You'll know how to work more effectively with people who don't speak English.

If you're a leader, you now know that your first action is to educate your team about differences and set the example. Find your pilot fish—the people who can tell you what you need to know—*good or bad*—so that you can lead most effectively. Don't shy away from constructive conflict—it's often when the most incredible breakthroughs occur. Don't let naysayers and derailers make you question your path—you know that learning to work with people not like you isn't just the right thing, it's essential for your business.

Expand the pool of talent you recruit from so that you have more diverse candidates at the beginning of—and throughout—the hiring process, and you'll end up with a better team, not just a more diverse one.

You're ahead. You're out in front of this new world we live and work in. You're ahead of your competitors and you're likely ahead of most of the people you work with. You can show them the way and be the example for how to effectively work with all kinds of people, even those you don't like much. Business isn't about dealing with the world the way you want the world to be—it's about *dealing with the world the way the world is*. Ready or not, the world—and the workplace—are changing quickly. But you read this book. You're ready.

Index